Korean Cuisine

Korean Cuisine

An Illustrated History

Michael J. Pettid

REAKTION BOOKS

Published by Reaktion Books Ltd
33 Great Sutton Street
London EC1V 0DX
www.reaktionbooks.co.uk

First published 2008

Printed and bound in China

British Library Cataloguing in Publication Data
Pettid, Michael J.
    Korean cuisine : an illustrated history
    1. Food habits – Korea – History   2. Food habits – Korea
    3. Cookery – Korea – History   4. Cookery, Korean
    I. Title
    394.1'2'09519

ISBN–13: 978 1 86189 348 2

Contents

Introduction

The Korean is omnivorous. Birds of the air, beasts of the field, and fish from the seas, nothing comes amiss to his palate. Dog-meat is in great request at certain seasons; pork and beef with the blood undrained from the carcase; fowls and game – birds cooked with the lights, giblets, head and claws intact, fish, sun-dried and highly malodorous, all are acceptable to him.

Angus Hamilton[1]

The world grows smaller each day. With the processes of globalization and the diffusion of information, the planet seems to shrink; yet one effect is that we are becoming increasingly aware of other cultures, no matter where we might live. A wonderful consequence of this is the spread of various food cultures around the world. This allows us in the twenty-first century to sample foods from many places that we may never have the opportunity to visit and cultures that we may never explore deeply. And food is an excellent window to a culture: what better means could there be to understand how people live?

What comes to mind when we think of Korea? This, of course, depends on where one stands, one's background and so forth. One might think of a divided country; economic prowess; perhaps recent sporting events. But beyond these, what is the strongest image of Korea? Perhaps Korean food is one item that should be considered. *Kimch'i, pulgogi* or a number of other dishes are known outside of Korea – foods that have some mystique to the non-Korean and might seem strange or, at the very least, different.

The foods of Korea are often approached with either a degree of fear or trepidation by visitors to the country. Commonly heard

Pulgogi, thinly sliced, marinated beef.

Chinese cabbage (*paech'u*) *kimch'i*, the most common variety of *kimch'i* today.

remarks are that the food is overwhelmed by the taste of garlic and chilli pepper, that it is all *kimch'i*, or that it is simply not for non-Koreans. Many a non-Korean will quickly turn up his or her nose at the mere mention of the word *kimch'i* without realizing that there are over two hundred varieties of this fermented dish, with a wide range of flavours. We also are treated in the Western media to the occasional diatribe on the 'barbaric' practice of eating dog meat in Korea. However, is there discussion on *why* some Koreans eat dog meat? When the non-Korean is properly indoctrinated into the nuances and varieties of food in Korea, we rarely hear such generalizations or criticisms. Korean cuisine is diverse and cannot be characterized by a few seasonings such as garlic or chilli pepper any more accurately than Italian food by pasta, American food by the hot dog, or Chinese food by chop suey.

There is also the other side of Korean food, perhaps most commonly championed by Koreans, as being a very healthy cuisine. The liberal use of soybeans, many vegetable dishes, herbs with curative or preventive properties and moderate amounts of meats certainly seem to make the cuisine fall on the healthy side of the ledger, but is this entirely true? This too is simply another aspect of some, not all, Korean cuisine.

As one comes to look at Korean foods, the bond between what Koreans have historically eaten and the culture of Korea becomes vividly apparent. The terrain of the Korean peninsula, climatic aspects

Chŏlp'yŏn ttŏk. White rice cakes and those made with mugwort (*ssuk*).

and the flora and fauna have undoubtedly been factors in the creation of Korean cuisine. So too have worldviews such as Buddhism and Confucianism. The bonds between food and the physical and mental cultures of Korea are inseparable. There is simply no division between Korea, Koreans and the cuisine of Korea.

'Cuisine' is defined as the manner in which cultures manipulate and transform potential foodstuffs into what these cultures consider proper human foods.[2] Thus, what makes Korean foods 'Korean' includes the detailed processes that Koreans use to transform various raw materials into food that is culturally considered to have been prepared correctly. In conjunction with the manner of preparing food are the cultural practices that determine what can, or cannot, be eaten, the manner in which meals are taken, and the social significance attached to various foods. It is no small wonder that what we eat plays such a significant role in our lives.

Until very recently in human history, most human activities revolved around securing sufficient food.[3] This allows us to understand the reasons for humans placing such a great emphasis on food and its proper preparation. At the start, it is not money, political power or sex that makes human societies go, but rather food. By examining historical food culture in Korea, we will gain a better understanding of part of what makes Koreans 'Korean' and how a very distinctive food culture has developed to the present day.

A Brief History of Korea

We cannot begin to really consider Koreans and their food culture without a basic understanding of the historical events that have shaped the peoples living on and around the Korean peninsula over the past several millennia. While our knowledge of Paleolithic and Neolithic humans is fragmentary and constantly changing at best, archaeological research has allowed us to understand that by the mid- to late Neolithic period (roughly 6,000 BCE–1,000 BCE) the inhabitants of the Korean peninsula had begun to practice rudimentary agriculture along with ongoing hunting and gathering activities. The presence of geometric-patterned pottery ('comb' pattern pottery; *pitsal muni t'ogi*) dating from about 3,000 BCE demonstrates that these early peoples had become somewhat settled and such a situation would have permitted the practice of basic agrarian activities.[4]

Tan'gun, the legendary founder of Kojosŏn. This statue has been officially approved by the Ministry of Culture and Tourism and is located at Sajik-tan in Seoul.

Ssuk growing wild.

Moving forward, documentation of the peoples living on and around the Korean peninsula becomes far clearer. Current evidence suggests that the Bronze Age began around the first millennium BCE on the Korean peninsula, accompanied by the formation of walled-town states. While the exact dating of these various states is difficult at best, by the fourth century BCE the polities had developed to the point that their existence is noted in Chinese records.[5] One of the first of these early polities was the kingdom of Kojosŏn (that is, Old Chosŏn), thought to have been located around the Taedong River basin near modern-day P'yŏngyang of North Korea.

One of the most interesting aspects of Kojosŏn is the foundation myth of this kingdom, known as the Myth of Tan'gun (*Tan'gun sin-hwa*).[6] This short myth tells of Hwanung, the son of the heavenly god, coming to the human world and fathering a son with a bear transformed into a woman. The offspring of this union was Tan'gun, the mythical founder of Kojosŏn. Most revealing in the myth are the aspects that show how people lived at this time. First, when Hwanung descends to the human world he brings with him the ability to control the wind, rain and clouds, clearly alluding to his ability to manage the elements that govern agriculture. Thus, we can understand that Kojosŏn was primarily an agrarian society. Second, in the process of transforming to a human, the bear is required to eat nothing except mugwort (Kor. *ssuk*) and garlic for one hundred days. Here we can suspect that certain foods had already been acknowledged as having either medicinal or religious value by these early inhabitants of the Korean peninsula.

A Koguryŏ period tomb mural, located in Manchuria, depicts women serving food (Muyongch'ong [Tomb of the Dancers]).

In addition to mythology, archaeological finds help us understand some aspects of diet in ancient times. One of the most important of these is the large drawing on a rock at Pan'gudae, located in the south-eastern part of the peninsula, that depicts whales and other marine life, demonstrating the importance of fishing activities at this time. Further-more, archaeological excavations have found numerous shell mounds that reveal the diets of these ancient people were rich in various marine foods and also land animals such as wild boar and deer.[7] In addition to hunting and fishing activities, agriculture and livestock-rearing con-tributed to dietary needs.

Interaction with neighbouring states, particularly kingdoms in China, resulted in technological advances for the ancient Koreans. Most notable was the introduction of iron culture from China in the fourth century BCE, which permitted significant advances in agricul-ture. Sophisticated farming implements such as ploughshares and sickles have been unearthed from this time and show agriculture production was greatly increased. The ploughshares, whether pulled by animal or human labour, allowed much more land to be cultivated and iron sickles meant that rice and other grains were harvested in bunches rather than by individual stalks.[8] Food production in this time, then, experienced great increase.

The first century BCE until the seventh century CE in Korea is known as the Three Kingdoms period. Koguryŏ (37 BCE–668 CE) occupied the northern part of the Korean peninsula and much of Manchuria, Paekche (18 BCE–660 CE) was located in the southwestern portion of the peninsula, and Silla (57 BCE–935 CE) was based in the southeastern part of the peninsula. In actuality, there were more than just three kingdoms, with the Kaya kingdoms located in the southern part of the peninsula and the island kingdom of T'amna on Cheju Island. Each of these polities had its own cultural practices and unique foods. For example, Chinese records concerning Paekche inform us that the people of this kingdom had a special fondness for cold foods and for fermented foods such as *kimch'i*.[9] We can begin to understand the diversity in contemporary Korean regional foods as, in part, being founded in the cultural heterogeneity of the Three Kingdoms period.

This period was one of rapid development in terms of culture for all the kingdoms. Frequent interaction with China permitted the intro-duction of a writing system, legal systems and new worldviews. In particular, by the fourth century both Buddhism and Confucianism

Chin mandu.

had entered the Korean kingdoms and begun to alter the way the people understood their world. International exchange was hardly limited to China, though, as these early states interacted with ancient polities located on the Japanese archipelago, peoples to the north of the peninsula, and even quite distant places represented by Arabian and Central Asian traders.

Subsequent to the Three Kingdoms period was a period that is sometimes referred to as 'Unified Silla', but is more accurately described as the Northern and Southern Kingdom period. Silla was able to defeat Paekche and Koguryŏ and unify much of the southern portion of the peninsula. Refugees from Koguryŏ, however, founded a new kingdom to the north known as Parhae (Chin. Bohai, 698–926). While the relations between these two states were initially acrimonious, with time they settled into a more or less peaceful coexistence. Culturally, both polities embraced Buddhism, as indeed all of the states of the Three Kingdoms period had long done in addition to their indigenous belief systems. They also maintained an array of international contacts.

The first unification of the Korean peninsula occurred with the advent of the Koryŏ dynasty (918–1392) in the early tenth century. This polity arose from the political turmoil in the ninth century when Silla had significantly decayed and the Parhae kingdom had collapsed. This dynasty can be characterized as having great admiration for the culture of Sung China on one hand, and as seeing itself as politically equal with China on the other hand. It was also a state with numerous international contacts and hosted merchants from as far away as the Middle East. Kaesŏng, the capital city of the dynasty, was a bustling international port linked to the Yellow Sea by river and developed as a commerce centre for the country. Through its international contacts, Koryŏ became known in the Western world, albeit in a limited fashion, and the modern name 'Korea' is derived from this dynasty.

Koryŏ had the misfortune to experience the invasion of the Mongols in the thirteenth century. While this period of invasion and subsequent occupation was a tragedy that resulted in much loss of life and hardship, it was a period in which the vast reach of the Mongol empire was brought into the Korean peninsula. Specifically, various foods that are now considered as 'traditional' Korean foods, such as *mandu* (a stuffed dumpling) and the many popular grilled meat dishes, were introduced during this period, along with noodle dishes and seasonings such as black pepper.

Late in the fourteenth century Koryŏ gave way to a new dynasty named Chosŏn (1392–1910). Most of our images of pre-modern Korea are of life in Chosŏn: this was a time of great change and scientific innovation. Not a few of these changes were in terms of agriculture and significantly altered the diet of the people. Social institutions underwent change too, particularly with the adoption of Song dynasty Confucianism as the official ideology of the country.

It is, however, incorrect to view Chosŏn as a static or culturally monolithic period. This dynasty spanned some five hundred years, and life in early Chosŏn was very different from life in late Chosŏn. Chronological proximity causes us to view the late Chosŏn as the embodiment of this time period, but by using historical records we can easily understand that there were significant differences between early and late Chosŏn.

When discussing the major events that shaped Chosŏn, we should begin with the appropriation of Confucianism as the guiding ideology for society. Simply put, Confucianism was a system for the ordering the country by extending basic human hierarchal relations such as those dictated in the Five Cardinal Relations and the Three Bonds. The Five Cardinal Relationships (Kor. *oryun*) are affection between father and son, justice between ruler and subject, distinction between husband and wife, hierarchy between senior and junior and trust between friends. The Three Bonds (Kor. *samgang*) refer to the defining

Sajik-tan, established in 1394, is where the kings of Chosŏn offered yearly rites and grain to the gods of the earth on behalf of the people.

qualities in relationships between ruler and subject (loyalty), children to parents (filial piety), and husband and wife (distinction in terms of duty). These basic building blocks were extended to the entire government structure and utilized to order society by the ruling elites of Chosŏn. As such, Chosŏn became a quite rigid society based upon social privilege and responsibility.

At the pinnacle of Chosŏn society were those who held *yangban* status. Only male members of this status group, based on lineage and birthright, could take the government service examinations that allowed access to the Chosŏn officialdom. Below this status group were the so-called middle people (*chung'in*) who functioned as the technocrats in the Chosŏn bureaucracy. Next were freeborn commoners, or the great bulk of the tax-paying peasantry, the cultivators of food. Finally came the lowborn, which group included slaves, entertainers, butchers and shamans. While these status groups were not absolutely static, it was exceedingly difficult for those in the lower strata of society to move upwards.

Of course, Confucianism was not the only belief system in Chosŏn. Buddhism, although officially proscribed by the Confucian elites, continued to play an important role in the lives of the people as did the shamanic worldview. Moreover, age-old folk practices never lost importance in the customs of the people. Thus, Chosŏn society had many cultural influences notwithstanding the government support of Confucianism as orthodoxy.

One aspect of Confucianism that is important to this study is its emphasis on scholarship. Such stress resulted in an outpouring of scientific innovation in the dynasty and a good portion of this was related to improving agricultural practices. One important development in the fifteenth century was the invention of rain gauges and the system of conducting regular readings to determine if the upcoming crop would be sufficient.[10]

Agricultural productivity was an area of concern to the government of Chosŏn and thus various resources were directed to this end. One aspect of this was publishing books on farming techniques. An early example was the 1429 publication of *Nongsa chiksŏl* ('Straight Talk on Farming') that outlined methods for improving agricultural output. Publications such as *Nongsa chiksŏl* continued throughout the Chosŏn period and helped improve agrarian yields. The peasant farmer class used fertilizers to increase yields and began to transplant rice seedlings (rather than directly sowing seed) more widely to fully utilize land.[11] Finally, hundreds of reservoirs were constructed as a means to combat drought and a grain loan system was established to provide aid to farmers in difficult times. Such improvements led to markedly increased agricultural production in Chosŏn compared to earlier times.

From 1592–8 Chosŏn suffered a series of devastating invasions from Japan, and in 1627 and 1636 two separate invasions by the Manchu people. Aside from the tremendous loss of life resulting from these invasions, the country also moved in a new direction in the aftermath, whether intended or not. In the second half of Chosŏn, some groups put an increasing emphasis on practical innovation and accepting advances in technology and agriculture from outside the country. The men most often associated with this innovation are now grouped as *sirhak* (practical learning) scholars. With the fall of the Ming dynasty (1368–1644) and the advent of the Manchu Qing dynasty (1644–1911) in China, Chosŏn's wholly China-centred view underwent significant change, and the *sirhak* scholars sought innovative ways to improve the lot of the country through bettering the economic, legal and agrarian systems.

In the post-invasions period, the country began to experience transformations in its economic structure due to the government's lessening

Chilli peppers are one of the 'new' foods introduced to Korea from the Americas in the mid-Chosŏn period.

the tax burden on peasants, which indirectly allowed the growth of commercial development. Specifically, there was great growth in the number of periodic markets, generally held every five days. These markets numbered around one thousand by the nineteenth century and were centres of both commerce and entertainment. Coupled with the growth of domestic markets was increased trade with China and Japan, all of which gave rise to a merchant class and the start of a trade economy.

In agriculture, there was further innovation in irrigation techniques that allowed double-cropping in parts of the country. Also, in 1662 a government office was established to oversee building and maintaining reservoirs and in 1778 a comprehensive plan was promulgated to maintain the irrigation system countrywide; by the end of the eighteenth century there were over 6,000 reservoirs in use.[12] As peasant farmers could produce more crops than they needed for self-consumption or tax requirements, they used portions of their lands to grow cash crops. In the later half of Chosŏn numerous new crops from the Americas were introduced to Korea via China, Japan, Europe and the Philippines such as corn, potatoes, sweet potatoes, chilli peppers, tomatoes, peanuts, squash and tobacco. Some of these crops – particularly potatoes and sweet potatoes – could be grown in soils and terrains that heretofore had not been utilized for agriculture, such as hillsides and rocky soils. Others were important cash crops that could be used for trade to obtain other necessities. In short, this was a time of tremendous change in agriculture in Korea.

By the nineteenth century the long-standing world order of East Asia began to crumble. Western countries had begun serious efforts to open the Asian countries to trade, with both China and Japan entering into unequal trade treaties with Western countries by the 1860s. Chosŏn could not hope to escape this. After Japan forced Chosŏn into opening ports for trade in 1876, there ensued a series of treaties with Western countries such as the United States followed by Britain, France and others. Most of these treaties ensured the Western countries the right to trade in Chosŏn and to spread Christianity. However, it was Japan that would ultimately topple the Chosŏn dynasty and assert its imperialistic goals on Korea.

As the Chosŏn dynasty struggled through its last century, there was increasing pressure to open the country up to trade from the West, China, and Japan. Along with external pressure, internally the country suffered from a number of rebellions, the most significant of which was the Tonghak Rebellion of 1894. It was not really a matter of Chosŏn falling, but rather which country would colonize Korea. In the end, this was Japan, and for thirty-six years (1910–45) Koreans suffered greatly under the yoke of Japan's imperialism. While this period is a dark one in Korea's history, it was also a period of great change and transformation. These changes were largely for the benefit of Japan, but Koreans did witness a great deal of modernization during this time.

In terms of food production, the colonial period was one that marked a major break from earlier times. One result was the large-scale loss of land owned by Koreans to the Japanese colonial government and its organs. One consequence of this was larger-scale farming designed for export to Japan. Secondly, while rice production increased significantly, this was not aimed at Koreans, but rather providing rice to the Japanese home market.[13] Koreans had less rice available and consequently the production of other grains such as millet rose. Thirdly, long-standing customs such as brewing alcohol at home ceased in this time as large-scale breweries were opened and mass-produced spirits.[14] Finally, processed foods such as instant noodles became increasingly common, as did foods of Western origins, such as bread.

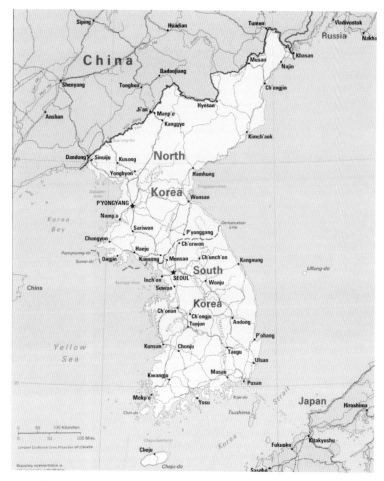

Map of the Korean peninsula.

The colonial period ended with Japan's defeat in World War II, but Korea did not receive the liberation its people had hoped for. Rather, a series of events tied to the international political struggle known as the Cold War led to the division of Korea into North and South, and eventually the Korean War (1950–53). It was not until the industrialization of the 1960s that South Korea was able to rise from these catastrophic circumstances and begin the building that has led to it becoming a global economic power in the present day.

Geography and Climate

The geographic and climatic conditions of the Korean peninsula have had much influence in the development of Korean cuisine and the cultural practices surrounding food. The nature of the Korean peninsula itself has allowed for easy contact with other cultures through either marine or land contacts. The size of the peninsula is not large at about 223,000 km² – in comparison, Great Britain is roughly 230,000 km² – with South Korea accounting for about 99,000 km². The northern reaches of the peninsula border Russia and the People's Republic of China, to the east is the East Sea (usually cited as the Sea of Japan in Western atlases), to the west the Yellow Sea and to the south the East China Sea. The peninsula is approximately 1,000 kilometres from north to south, and ranges from about 200 kilometres across at its narrowest point to 320 kilometres across at its widest. Dotting the coastal waters are some 3,300 islands, about 200 of which are inhabited, with the vast majority located either to the south or west of the peninsula. The largest of the islands is Cheju Island, a volcanic island located at the closest point about 140 km to the south of the peninsula, of approximately 1,860 km² (for comparison, the Hawaiian island of Maui is 1,886 km²).

If one was to characterize the general terrain of Korea, mountainous would be the most appropriate adjective. Indeed, some 70 per cent of the peninsula is covered by mountains, with the main mountain range being the T'aebaek Range, which runs along the east coast and stretches over some 500 kilometres. The mountains of the peninsula are not particularly high, with the highest being Mt Paektu, located on the border of North Korea and China, at 2,744 metres. In the South, Mt Chiri (1,915 metres) in the southwestern part of the peninsula and Mt Halla (1,950 metres) on Cheju Island are the two highest peaks.

The animals found in the mountains of the Korean peninsula are largely the same as those in Manchuria and the northern reaches of China. Historically, large carnivores including black bears and tigers roamed the mountainous regions of the peninsula, but these days the tiger is extinct and bear sightings relatively rare. Wolves, foxes, wild boar, deer, rabbits and squirrels were all once common in rural areas and were hunted, but today have experienced greatly reduced numbers due to human encroachment on their habitats.

The waters that border the peninsula have provided Koreans with an excellent source of food. The peninsula tilts downwards towards the

Pollack roe (*msŏngnan chŏt*).

Yellow Sea, which is so named because of its colour; rivers carry yellow mud, known as loess, into the sea. This is a shallow body of water with an average depth of only 44 metres, but a tremendously rich source of marine life including porpoises, croaker, Spanish mackerel and Pacific herring. Moreover, the wide range of tides along the western Korean coast create huge tidal flats – among the largest in the world – with every outgoing tide, and from these flats are harvested numerous marine life such as the tiny and salty shrimp that are used to season numerous foods.[15] Other shellfish are also harvested in the Yellow Sea such as clams, oysters, abalone and sea-snails.

In stark contrast to the shallow Yellow Sea is the East Sea, which runs along the eastern coast of the peninsula. The average depth of this sea is 1,361 metres, and it is over 3,700 metres at its deepest point. The continental shelf on this sea is shallow and tides are just over a metre high, thus offering a very different marine environment from the Yellow Sea. Squid, yellowtail, whales, dolphin and various types of mackerel are among the commonly caught species.

To the south of the peninsula lies the East China Sea, called the South Sea (*Nam hae*) by Koreans. Historically, since this sea contains hundreds of islands, it was called the Sea of Many Islands (*Tado hae*). The irregular shape of the coast and the many islands result in over 4,600 kilometres of Korean coastline on this sea. The main harvest here includes anchovies, hairtail, shark, mackerel, squid, flounder, octopus and mullet, among other species. Numerous shellfish are also taken from these waters.

Along with the saltwater fish contributing to the diets of Koreans are the numerous freshwater fish found in the many rivers and lakes on the peninsula. In comparison to the relatively small size of the peninsula, Korea boasts six rivers over 400 kilometres in length, with the longest being the northern Amnok (commonly called the Yalu) at 790 kilometres; in the southern parts of the peninsula, the Han River (514 km) and the Naktong River (525 km) are the two longest rivers. Among the fish caught in these rivers are types of eel, carp and catfish.

The Korean peninsula is located in a transitional zone between the continental landmass of north-east Asia and the arc of islands that line the western Pacific Ocean. The parts of the peninsula along the Yellow Sea are subject to the weather influences of continental Asia, especially the winter climate. The east coast, however, is sheltered from this by the T'aebaek Mountain Range. The seasonal changes on the peninsula are distinct and characterized by cold winters, particularly west of the T'aebaek Mountain Range, hot and humid summers and relatively dry and clear spring and autumn seasons. Annual precipitation is about 1,500 mm in the central parts of the peninsula, with more than half of

Papsang, a table with numerous side-dishes.

this falling in the summer. The presence of heavy rain during the hot summer growing season has allowed Korea to be an ideal locale for rice cultivation.

Food Culture in Korea

The historical and geographic backdrop has heavily influenced the foods developed as part of Korean cuisine. Historical interaction with peoples in northern and eastern Asia has greatly added to the foods available to those living on the peninsula. Likewise, the introduction of foods from distant lands such as the Americas helped shape the distinctive forms of Korean cuisine that developed during the eighteenth century. Along with outside influences, internal compartmentalization caused by the mountainous terrain fostered the growth and maintenance of local specializations in both menu and processing methods. Even today we can note distinct regional variations in Korean cuisine.

The production of sufficient food was nearly always a concern, either for the farmers who tilled the land or the governments that collected taxes and managed the country based on agrarian output. An old saying, 'eating is heaven' (*mŏgnŭn kŏsi hanŭl ida*) well expresses the importance of food. If the people were well-fed, there was certainly less reason for rebellion or dissatisfaction with the rulers. Thus, agricultural production – particularly of grains such as rice – was always a major concern for the governments of pre-modern Korea.

While we cannot pinpoint the start of rice cultivation in Korea with certainty, we do know that it has long been a staple food for the peoples on the Korean peninsula. The predominant grain before the introduction of rice was millet and, even after the start of rice farming, it remained an important grain. The range of dates that scholars indicate for the introduction of rice extends from around the first millennium BCE to the first century BCE; there are even claims in recent years that push the introduction of rice to the peninsula as early as the fourteenth century BCE, although this is not widely accepted. Despite this inexact dating of the introduction of rice, we do know with certainty that rice quickly became an essential part of Korean cuisine. Rice is excellent for eating as both a whole grain and as flour, and this led to the development of a variety of foods based on it.

As noted above, the ocean provided Koreans with a steady supply of food, and as a means to preserve the items harvested from the seas,

Young rice plants.

elaborate methods of drying and fermenting marine goods were developed with considerable differences from region to region. Numerous seaweeds were also harvested from the ocean.

As there is a dearth of pasture lands on the peninsula, stock farming was only practiced on a small scale in pre-modern times. The livestock that was raised included cattle, pigs and chickens; however, the meat of these animals was a rare treat for commoners or the low-born. Other meats were used in moderation, including dog and wild animals such as deer, boar and pheasant, while that of goats or sheep was utilized for medicines more often than food.

The many mountains of the peninsula provided a broad selection of wild plants and herbs. Very intricate and sophisticated methods of identification, preparation and storage for these important foodstuffs were developed and gave the people variety both in taste and in nutrition. As a means to provide vegetables all year round, a fermented vegetable dish known as *kimch'i* was developed early on in Korean history. The cultivation of vegetables was also common and added to the diversity of diets in pre-modern times.

Another key element of Korean cuisine is the long-standing understanding of the close relationship between food and health. Old sayings such as, 'Food is medicine' (*ŭmsigi kot yagi toenta*) reflect a strong consciousness of what modern science tells us today: our health is intimately related with what we eat. Consequently, within Korean food culture, numerous foods and drinks are associated with various medicinal properties. Moreover, certain common foods and drinks are often supplemented with ingredients such as ginseng, honey, cinnamon, ginger and so on in the hope of providing the body with healthy nutrients.

Keeping the above factors in mind, the next few chapters will closely examine the types of foods that were enjoyed by Koreans in premodern times. As much as possible, this volume will seek to provide a broad understanding of the many foods enjoyed in past times and demonstrate the diversity of what can be called Korean cuisine by including regional specializations. More than simply food, the cultural importance of food and its social utility will be a focal point of this work. As stated above, food is a critical element in the formation of any culture and one that will allow a better understanding of cultural and social practices.

1   Daily Foods

Dinner tables in our country are arranged with five side-dishes.
First, in the centre of the row furthest from the diner is a fresh,
uncooked vegetable, such as radish, lettuce, chives or herbs. To the
left of this is placed a parboiled vegetable; radish, eggplant or *tŏdŏk* is
cut thinly and stir fried. To the right is placed a seasoned vegetable;
radish, eggplant, or wild parsley is first put into brine and then
well-seasoned. Next, in the centre row to the left is a dried vegetable
or dried fish that is lightly fried; to the right is *kim'chi*. *Kimch'i* is a
vegetable that is soaked in salty water, seasoned and then fermented
for a period of time. To the inside, closest to the diner are placed
a spoon and chopsticks; this is what is known as a 'five side-dish
table.' When guests are invited, each is prepared such a table . . .
After the table is so arranged and presented, rice, soup and soy
sauce are brought out. Next, soups made with fish or meat and a
vegetable soup is served; then, broiled fish or meat is served. When
there are many meat dishes as many as seven or eight dishes are
served, whereas other times only one or two are served.[1]

The above, written by Cho Sin (1454–1528), describes an ideal meal. But
is such a lavish meal really what Koreans ate as everyday fare in past
times? Both then and now, the ideal daily meal in Korean cuisine con-
sists of rice, a soup or stew and numerous side dishes. Of course, this
was not always possible as the availability of foods, social status and
economic means played large roles in the foods that people were able to
eat. As we will see, Cho's ideal meal was in reality not something that
most Koreans would have enjoyed regularly; it was only available to the
uppermost classes, and even then not enjoyed daily.

This painting entitled *Sŏnmyojo chejae kyŏngsuyŏn-to* ('Banquet for the Aged Mothers of Ministers at King Sŏnjo's Court, 1605') shows preparations for a banquet. Note the male cooks preparing the food.

Before examining the various elements of daily foods, it will be helpful to cover the basic components of Korean meals. First is rice. The rice eaten in Korea is a medium grain variety similar to that of Japan. When properly cooked it is slightly sticky, but not to the extent that the individual grains lose their shape. While rice was not always available to those of lower status groups, it was an ideal component of

Papsang, a meal with side-dishes, meats and a stew.

any meal. Often it would be mixed with other grains such as barley or millet in order to stretch supplies. For those of lower-status groups in pre-modern times, rice might have been completely supplanted by another, less desirable, grain such as barley or millet. Nonetheless, the importance of rice to Korean cuisine can be seen in that the word for cooked rice, *pap*, is also a term for a full meal.

Korean notions of social status are well reflected in the terminology for taking a meal. In general usage, *pap* is the term for a meal, but when served to one's elders, the honorific term *chinji* is used. In past times, when meals were served to the king or queen, the word *sura* was used, and when rice was served during ancestral rites, the word *chenme* or *me* was utilized. In conjunction with the special terms for meals, honorific verbs for 'eating' were used. In many ways, the intricate social relations found in Korean culture are seen in the common practice of taking meals.

No Korean meal is complete without an array of vegetables, served either as separate side dishes (known as *panch'an*) or added to soups and stews. In fact, meals are generally classified by the number of side dishes (*chŏp*) served at a meal: typically, there are three-, five-, seven-, nine- or twelve-dish meals. Vegetables can be eaten cooked or raw, seasoned or unseasoned, depending upon the dish. Vegetables found in

P'a kimch'i, kimch'i made with spring onions.

Korean meals can be either those cultivated in fields, such as squash or chilli peppers, or the numerous wild plants and herbs collected from the mountains. The proliferation of vegetables in Korean cuisine is partly a result of the environment of the peninsula, which allows a considerable number of plants to grow in the wild, and partly owing to the conditions in past times such as war or famine that caused people to look for alternative foods, and the vegetarian fare that dominated the Buddhist Koryŏ dynasty and diets of Buddhists thereafter.

Essential to any Korean meal is *kimch'i*, a type of food made by salting and seasoning certain vegetables such as cabbage and radish. As these vegetables contain a great deal of water, they are difficult to store for long periods of time. This problem led to the development of fermentation methods for vegetables as a means of preservation. There are many, many types of *kimch'i*, from the now-common variety, made with Chinese cabbage, to those made with radishes, spring onions and other ingredients. Ingredients added for seasoning include salt, seafood, chilli powder and a type of fermented seafood known as *chŏtkal*.

The condiments and seasonings used to provide flavour to vegetables and other foods are also essential in Korean cuisine. Basic condiments such as soy sauce (*kanjang*), soybean paste (*toenjang*) and red chilli pepper paste (*koch'ujang*) were kept in large quantities by each household, as they were necessary for providing the range of different tastes and seasonings found in foods. Along with providing foods with flavour, these condiments were important sources of protein in the diets of pre-modern Korea. Other seasonings, such as the aforementioned *chŏtkal* and black pepper, were also important for flavouring and preserving foods.

Along with rice, vegetables, *kimch'i* and condiments, Korean cuisine often features meat or fish side-dishes and a soup or stew. While beef dishes would have been a rare treat for most in pre-modern times, fish dishes would have been more commonplace. Unlike some Western cuisines, however, the meat dishes would have been a secondary element in the meal and served in relatively small portions. Stews and soups also would have been served as a complement to the main meal of rice and side-dishes.

In general, Korean meals tend to emphasize a harmony between flavours, colours, textures and temperatures. Grains like rice have much more delicate flavours than heavily seasoned vegetables or stews, and this provides a balance in flavour. Colours of vegetables, meats and grains are also important in considering a properly set table. Diversity in texture is found in the different side-dishes, dried and fresh foods and even in rice mixed with other grains. Temperature contrast is found in cool foods such as *kimch'i* and hot foods such as soups and cooked rice. More than a single flavour or texture, the success of a Korean meal is determined by the overall harmony of divergent sensations found in it.

The three main condiments in Korean cuisine: clockwise from the top, *kang-jang*, *koch'ujang* and *toenjang*.

A tray with various *namul*. In the centre is *koch'ujang* paste. These are subsequently mixed with rice and eaten.

Grains and Legumes

> Wrap the rice in lotus leaves, do not prepare any other side-dishes;
> I have on my hat of green bamboo, bring me my raincoat of verdant rushes.
>
> Am I following the mindless white egret or is it following me?[2]

As soon as the ancient peoples living on and around the Korean peninsula began to settle and farm, the importance of grains was established in their diets. Such a value is even reflected in the foundation myths of early kingdoms such as Koguryŏ and T'amna. In the Koguryŏ (37 BCE–668 CE) foundation myth, Chumong, the founder of the kingdom, is said to have received barley seeds delivered by a pair of doves sent by his mother as soon as he established his kingdom.[3] In a similar vein, the three princesses who come to T'amna to wed the three founding deities of Cheju Island bring with them the seeds of the five grains; subsequently, the myth relays that after the princesses settled with the three men they planted the seeds and began to farm for the first time.[4] The prominence of grain in these myths reflects both the political and social significance of this food in early times.

While rice is perhaps what one imagines when thinking of grains in the Korean diet, in pre-modern times there were other grains that were equally important. Barley and millet were both staple foods. Also eaten were wheat, sorghum and buckwheat, along with soybeans and other legumes. As rice is not indigenous to the Korean peninsula, the first attempts at agriculture were most likely aimed at cultivating millet, which seems to have been present on the peninsula at an early time.[5]

Nonetheless, the supremacy of rice as the staple food was established early on in Korean history during the Three Kingdoms period (1st century BCE–7th century CE) in both the Silla and Paekche kingdoms. As these kingdoms were located in the southern parts of the peninsula, the conditions for growing rice were favourable and allowed rice-farming to become more widespread. In the Greater Silla period (668–935 CE), rice was the most important staple grain and was collected as taxes. Etymologists note that the Sino-Korean word for 'tax' is a compound partly composed of the character for rice plant, and that this usage began in Korea during the Silla period.[6] The lives of the people and their rulers certainly were bound to the cycle of planting, weeding and harvesting, as the following poem written by Yi Kyubo (1168–1241) vividly describes:

Doubled over in the paddies, weeding rice plants in the rain;
Such a mud-smeared face, how can this be human?
Princes of the royal family do not hold me with contempt,
Your wealth and extravagances all arise from me.

The verdant-leaved new grains still not ripe,
[Yet] the village officials have already [begun] to press for taxes.
Ploughed by [our] vigour, the country's wealth stems from us;
How can they abuse us as such, will [they] strip our skin [also]?[7]

Such an emphasis on rice continued through the Chosŏn dynasty, when new methods of cultivation and varieties of rice were introduced and helped to significantly increase production.

Although at present the most common way of eating rice is on its own, it has long been the practice to combine rice with other grains such as millet, barley and sorghum, or even legumes, such as beans. In

Brown rice.

pre-modern times eating pure white rice was impossible for most, as it would have been prohibitively expensive. The adage, 'Thanks to ancestor rites, one can eat rice' (*chesa tŏg-e ssal pabida*), demonstrates the relative uncommonness of eating rice among lower social groups. This saying shows that rice was reserved for special occasions such as ancestor rites, rather than being daily fare. Thus, various seasonal grains, herbs, nuts and berries were commonly mixed in with rice. Rice is also eaten as gruel, often mixed with other grains or even meat or shellfish. Rice flour is used to make numerous types of rice cake known as *ttŏk*, over two hundred varieties in all. Some of the more popular varieties are *siru ttŏk* (steamed rice cakes), *kaep'i ttŏk* (cinnamon rice cakes) and *songp'yŏn* (rice cakes steamed on pine needles). Finally, there are numerous rice wines, both filtered and unfiltered.

The method of cooking rice in an iron pot, called a *sot* or *musoe sot*, dates back at least to the reign of King Taemusin (18–44 CE) of the Koguryŏ kingdom. *Sot* have also been unearthed in Silla period tombs, demonstrating both the cultural importance of the implement and that rice was cooked in much the same manner as today.

White rice, that is, rice that is hulled and polished, was the preferred rice for meals. The first step for preparing rice was to winnow out the

Rice mixed with barley and red beans.

chaff, after which the hulled rice is washed several times in cold water. Uncooked rice is soaked in cold water for two to four hours before cooking. The rice is then put into the *sot* and water added until it covers the back of one's hand when placed upon the rice in the pot, roughly a rice-water ratio of 1:1.2. Until the rice begins to boil, high heat is maintained; once the rice boils, the heat is left on high for a moment, and then reduced to a low flame until all of the water is absorbed by the rice. At this point the rice is done. This method of cooking rice was highly praised by visitors to Chosŏn Korea, as seen in the comments by the Qing Chinese visitor Zhang Ying who wrote, 'The people of Chosŏn cook rice well; the grains of rice have lustre, softness and a delicate fragrance, and are evenly cooked in the pot . . . Cooking rice without such care is a waste of what has been bestowed by the heavens.'[8]

Notwithstanding the preference accorded to rice, in parts of pre-modern Korea rice could simply not be cultivated and some could not afford to eat it. A nineteenth-century writer commented on such a situation, stating, 'Those in the south are adept at cooking rice, while those in the north excel in cooking millet (*cho pab*); so too are the customs different.'[9] Yet this is an oversimplification, as many in the southern parts of the peninsula also did not eat pure rice, and thus dishes such as *pori pap* (barley cooked with or without rice) developed among the lower-status groups. In short, eating white rice for three meals a day remained out of reach for many Koreans, or, at the very least, was reserved for special occasions, until the last decades of the twentieth century.

Consequently, Korean cuisine has an abundance of dishes that mix rice with other grains such as the aforementioned *pori pap*. After

Onlookers watch rice being pounded for *ttŏk* as they wait in line to buy some. Scenes such as these are becoming more frequent as 'traditional' ways of making food become more popular.

cooking, the barley-rice mixture is served in bowls and topped with *yŏlmu kimch'i* (*kimch'i* made with young radishes) and other vegetables and seasoned with *koch'ujang* (red pepper paste) and *toenjang* (soybean paste). While this dish was once a staple of peasants, it is now highly prized as a speciality dish.

Barley was an extremely important grain in past times, and not just as a supplement for rice. From records in the *Samguk sagi* ('History of the Three Kingdoms') we know that barley was planted in the winter for harvest in early summer.[10] Spring was a time of great hardship for farmers, as winter stores were often depleted and the newly-planted crops were not ready for harvest. This period was known as the 'barley hump' (*porit kogae*), as one had to survive, or 'get over the hump', until the winter barley was ready for harvest. At times this was exceedingly difficult, as reflected in the adage, 'the barley hump is higher than a great mountain' (*porit kogae-ga t'aesan poda nop'ta*).

Rice mixed with beans (*k'ong pap*) was another means to stretch rice supplies and is also now common in many homes and restaurants. In general, black beans are used to make this dish and are soaked overnight to soften them before cooking them with rice. However, on the Harvest Festival (Ch'usŏk, the fifteenth day of the eighth lunar month), beans that are not quite fully ripened are added to the rice and cooked as is. This has become a special holiday dish for Ch'usŏk known as *ch'ŏngdae k'ong pap*. As beans are high in protein and provide fibre, they are nowadays recognized as a food with excellent nutritional value.

Another dish that mixes various grains and legumes with rice is *ogok pap* (five-grain rice), which combines rice, red beans, black beans, millet and sorghum. The exact ingredients of *ogok pap* can vary, with glutinous rice (*ch'apssal*) and other grains often being added to or substituted for the above ingredients. The finished dish is reddish-black rice with a savoury fragrance that is one of the most representative dishes of the first full moon of the lunar year (*Taeborŭm*) in Korea. This was commonly prepared the day before the holiday and eaten with nine vegetable dishes on *Taeborŭm*; this practice was believed to be a means of bringing about a good harvest of grains in the forthcoming year. Families would also share the *ogok pap* they prepared with neighbouring families as a way of bringing about good fortune and abundance in the year ahead. Finally, on *Taeborŭm* one would eat one's *ogok pap* in nine small portions, rather than two or three meals, as another means of securing good fortune.

Yak pap (medicinal rice), also known as *yak sik* (medicinal food), is another food that is strongly associated with holidays in Korea. The history of this food dates back to the Silla kingdom during the reign of King Soji (479–500 CE), when glutinous rice was offered to a crow that had saved the king's life by informing him of an assassin in wait.[11] An early nineteenth-century writer, when recounting this story, comments; 'Thus it is said in the world that we have *yak pap* and even until today, we observe this custom on holidays.'[12] Various Chosŏn-period recipes inform us that to make this dish, glutinous rice is steamed until the grains are fully done, and then before the rice cools, jujubes, chestnuts, sesame oil, honey and soy sauce are mixed with it. The whole mixture is then steamed again for seven or eight hours until it becomes a blackish colour.[13] In addition to the above ingredients, other recipes called for adding dried persimmons. Like the *ogok pap* described above, this was a festive food that was to be shared with neighbors and relatives alike, and added to the convivial atmosphere of *Taeborŭm*.

Two seemingly useless by-products of cooking rice – the burnt rice on the bottom of the *sot* and the leftover rice grains in the pot – are not wasted. The crisp, thin layer of rice on the bottom of the *sot* is called *nurungji* and is enjoyed as a tasty snack by both adults and children. Even more desirable is *sungnyung*, the broth that is created by adding a little water to the *sot* after removing the rice and boiling it; the remains of the rice with the water create a tasty soup that is often enjoyed after a meal. A record from the late Chosŏn period describes this as, 'After

The burnt layer of rice on the bottom of this stone bowl is eaten along with water at the end of the meal.

eating rice, water is added to the remaining rice [in the *sot*], boiled for a bit, and then drunk.'[14] *Sungnyung* generally marks the end of the meal, and also facilitates easy cleanup of the *sot*.

In recent years, the nutritional value of eating rice mixed with other grains or brown rice (*hyŏnmi*) has been contrasted to that of white rice, which has much of its nutritional value taken out through processing. In that the majority of Koreans in pre-modern times did not eat simply white rice, we can see that the pre-modern mixtures of rice were far healthier fare than the present day penchant for white rice alone. It is not surprising, then, that in recent years an increasing number of Koreans are eating rice mixed with other grains or brown rice, as society has a heightened awareness of the benefits of healthy diets. In a small way, the resurgence of various mixtures of rice and other grains demonstrates the wisdom of pre-modern foods that were less processed than many foods of the present.

A currently popular rice dish is *pipim pap*, rice mixed with vegetables. This dish probably developed from foods eaten by peasants when cooked rice, or other cooked grains, was mixed with whatever vegetables were on hand. Nowadays, it is prepared with cooked rice covered with cooked and seasoned vegetables such as spinach, mushrooms, sea tangle, carrots and bean sprouts, and also meat and egg. All the ingredients are then mixed, directly before eating, and seasoned with *koch'ujang* (red pepper paste) to taste. There are numerous variations on this dish and it is often served in a hot stone bowl that permits the mixture to continue to cook after being served.

Given the importance of rice in Korean cuisine, it is not surprising to find numerous legends related to rice in pre-modern Korean culture. One interesting folktale that is found throughout the Korean peninsula is a legend concerning a hole in a rock. The legend tells of a temple deep in the mountains that gained fame through a special rock; at each meal-time rice would flow from this rock in exact proportion to the number of people present at the temple. Accordingly, regardless of how many monks and visitors or how few, there was no need to worry about rice. However, there was one monk who thought that inside the rock there must be a great store of rice, which he coveted. He started to poke into the hole to get at this cache. But this was the undoing of the source of rice, as from this point forward the rock only yielded water.

The moral of the above story is one of greed on a couple of different levels. Firstly, we can note the lesson in the legend that one should not be greedy. Greed will easily undermine a community, and given the reciprocal labour relations required in rice-farming, we can understand the importance of not taking more than one's share. Secondly, the legend clearly reflects the Buddhist teachings concerning greed. In the Four Noble Truths of Buddhism, life is said to be suffering, and the cause of such suffering is greed. The greedy monk in the story certainly

Chŏnju-style *pibimpap* is famous throughout Korea. Here it is served with soup made with bean sprouts (*k'ong namul kuk*).

demonstrates the folly of greediness in this aspect. That this legend centres on rice reveals the high position that rice held in the people's minds of pre-modern Korea: rather than a rock spewing riches or meats, the rock in this legend gives rice.

Wheat and buckwheat were more common in the northern reaches of the peninsula where growing rice was difficult. Noodles, especially in and after the Koryŏ dynasty, were an important foodstuff made with these grains. Buckwheat was the more common grain in Koryŏ and is still the mainstay of noodle dishes such as *naengmyŏn*, a cold noodle soup enjoyed in the hot summer months. The production of wheat and buckwheat has always been relatively small when compared to rice, and thus noodle dishes in pre-modern times were considered as delicacies and eaten only on special occasions such as weddings or birthday celebrations. The association of the length of noodles with human longevity resulted in these dishes being considered felicitous foods bonded with good fortune.

While seemingly not as prominent as rice, soybeans have long been an essential part of Korean cuisine. These legumes are thought to be indigenous to the northern part of China or Manchuria, which means that early polities around the Korean peninsula would have cultivated these crops. Soybeans are an important source of protein; they have high protein content (38–45%) and are a complete protein, that is, one that provides significant amounts of all the essential amino acids required by the human body. Moreover, they are prized for their high oil content (20%).

Given such qualities, it is not surprising to find soybeans and soy by-products present in many types of Korean cuisine. Perhaps most important to the flavour of Korean foods are the seasonings made from soybeans: *toenjang* (soybean paste) and *kanjang* (soy sauce). Sprouts from soybeans (*k'ong namul*) are eaten as a side-dish or added to soups and stews, oil from soybeans is used in cooking and the powder from ground, dried beans is also used in various foods. There are many records of the early Korean kingdoms using soy products; moreover, the value of soy products is seen in a record from 683 CE stating that *toenjang* and *kanjang* were among the presents exchanged in a royal wedding.[15]

While soybeans have been present in Korean cuisine since the time of the earliest kingdoms, tofu (Kor. *tubu*) did not become a common food until the early part of the Chosŏn dynasty. Chinese records attribute the invention of this food to Liu An, King of Huainan during the Former Han dynasty (206 BCE–9 CE). The first mention of this food in

Korean records is found in the literary collection of Yi Saek (1328–1396).[16] An entry in the dynastic record from 1434 recounts that the Ming emperor sent some serving women to the Chosŏn court to prepare a variety of foods, one of which was tofu. This account states that all the dishes were harmonious and served beautifully, and that the means of preparing the tofu was even more exquisite.[17] Of all the foods that the women brought from the Ming court to Chosŏn, it was just tofu that was singled out for praise in this particular entry. It is thought that after this time, dishes featuring tofu became common at the palace and then were disseminated throughout society.

Other types of beans are also prominent in Korean food such as the small red adzuki bean that is featured in numerous foods such as *ttŏk*, porridge (*p'at chuk*), and mixed with rice. The popularity of this bean might stem not only from its good taste, but also the efficacy of the colour red in keeping away baneful influences. Folklore holds that red beans have special properties; for example, a widespread folktale tells of a winged baby general who rises to save the people, but is betrayed by his own parents and killed. His parents honor his dying wish and bury him along with five sacks each of red beans and soybeans. The red beans then sprout as red-clad soldiers and the soybeans as horses and the baby general is about to rise and lead them to victory, only to again suffer defeat, this time at the hands of the government forces. While this legend is a tragic tale of betrayal and the subjugation of the people's wishes against the ruling class, it also hints at the magical properties of beans.

While neither grains nor legumes, potatoes and sweet potatoes were important sources of nutrition in pre-modern Korea. These starchy tubers were introduced in the late Chosŏn period and become essential crops for locales where rice or other crops could not be cultivated. Sweet potatoes seem to have been introduced to Korea via Japan by 1763 at the latest, when records mention that this food was being cultivated in the southeastern part of the peninsula.[18] Potatoes show up at a later date – not until the early nineteenth century – and it is not clear how they were introduced to Korea. Despite a relative late start for both of these tubers, their ability to grow in rocky soils and harsh climates such as Kangwŏn Province made these prominent foodstuffs, and they became important as famine-relief foods.

Condiments and Seasonings

An old Korean saying states, 'Food is only as good as the *jang*' (soy-bean-based sauces). This might seem a bit of an exaggeration, but the distinctive tastes of Korean cuisine are largely the result of the condiments that are used in flavouring foods either individually or in combination. While there is sometimes the erroneous assumption by visitors to Korea that all foods are heavily seasoned with chilli peppers, garlic, *toenjang*, *kanjang* or salt, this is more the result of not sampling the full array of Korean cuisine than an actual fact. A late nineteenth-century gentlewoman traveller to Korea, Isabella Bird Bishop, wrote of Korean seasonings,

> Oil of sesamum [sesame] is largely used in cooking, as well as vinegar, soy, and other sauces of pungent and objectionable odors, the basis of most of them being capsicums and fermented rotten beans![19]

While she was clearly not enamoured with Korean tastes, it is proper to note that Korean cuisine has a tremendous range of flavours that reach from very delicate tastes of vegetables to the stronger flavours of *toenjang tchigae* (soybean paste stew) and *kimch'i*. Moreover, even among *kanjang* or *toenjang* there is a wide expanse of varieties and regional specialities, resulting in very distinctive flavours. An early nineteenth-century account in *Chŭngbo sallim kyŏngje* ('Farm management, supplemented and enlarged') demonstrates the importance given to the preparation of *jang*:

> *Jang* is the source of all flavours. If the taste of a house's *jang* is not good, even if there are good vegetables or flavourful meats, one cannot prepare good food. The household head must always keep in mind the fermentation of *jang*, and through this will be able to have well-aged and good *jang*.[20]

In a similar vein, Yi Pinghŏgak (1759–1824) in her *Kyuhap ch'ongsŏ* ('Encyclopaedia for Women's Daily Life') gives instructions on the best days to make *jang* and also the importance of having the *changdoktae*, the terrace where earthenware jars of soy sauce and other *jang* were kept, face in an auspicious direction, determined by the yearly calendar.[21] In this section, we will examine some of the many seasonings that flavour Korean foods.

There is probably no better place to start when describing Korean seasonings than the main soybean-derived seasonings, *toenjang* and *kanjang*. The suffix *-jang* means soybean sauce; *toenjang* denotes 'thick' soybean sauce and *kanjang* expresses 'salty' soybean sauce. The basic ingredient for both of these seasonings is *meju*, soybean malt made by boiling whole soybeans. After boiling the mixture, it is mashed and shaped into blocks, then put in a warm place and allowed to ferment. In past times, *meju* was generally cooked in late autumn and allowed to ferment until past the lunar New Year, some three months in all. The blocks are then soaked in large earthenware pots of brine to make the soybean sauce (*jang*), which is subsequently made into *toenjang* or *kanjang*.

Kanjang in Korea has three basic varieties: a strong-flavoured sauce with a dark colour (*chin kanjang*), a medium-flavoured sauce with a light brown colour (*chung kanjang*), and a weak-flavoured sauce with a light, clear colour (*mulgŭn kanjang*). *Chin kanjang* requires at least five years of fermentation and due to its sweet flavour and dark colour it is used for boiling, fermenting or as a seasoning in *yak pap* (medicine rice) and in gruels. *Chung kanjang* was used in pastimes as a seasoning for vegetables or stews, while *mulgŭn kanjang*, with a one- to two-year fermentation period, was mainly used as a seasoning in soups.

Given the importance of *kanjang*, it is no wonder that recipe books of the Chosŏn period offer dozens of variations on this seasoning.[22] Great care was also afforded to the preparation of *kanjang* in each household, and the steps for making the seasoning were carefully followed according to family tradition. If a daughter-in-law failed to capture the correct taste of her husband's household's particular *kanjang*, it was considered a bad omen for the family. Many families even went so far as to offer small rituals to the household gods when making *kanjang* as a means to appease the gods and ensure a successful batch. Other customs such as hanging gold-coloured thread, traditional socks or red peppers – all thought to repel malevolent spirits – around the earthenware pots of *kanjang* were done to keep malicious spirits at bay.

In the twentieth century during the colonial period, Japanese-style soy sauce was introduced to Korea and mass-produced in factories. However, the flavour of the Japanese soy sauce did not match the Korean people's expectations and despite the rationing of crops for the military, Koreans continued to make their traditional *kanjang*, thus preserving this important element of Korean cuisine.

Closely related to the process of making *kanjang* is *toenjang*. One method of making this paste is to add salt to the leftover *meju* after removing the *kanjang* from the earthenware pot and allowing the mixture to ferment. The other method is simply to add brine to *meju* and ferment the mixture for about two months. There are numerous variations to these basic recipes, especially in adding boiled soybeans to the mixture; other types of *toenjang* include those adding rice, barley, wheat and other grains to create special flavours. There are literally dozens of varieties of *toenjang* that are enjoyed with specific foods and in certain seasons of the year. An interesting regional variation of *toenjang* specific to the south-western city of Naju is to grind fermented *meju* into a powder and then mix in steamed glutinous rice. This is allowed to sit overnight and then eggplants, cucumbers and chilli pepper leaves are mixed in. The entire mixture is then fermented in a warm place for several days. The result is a very unique *toenjang* that provides a substantial difference from the basic variety described above.

The medicinal and curative properties attributed to *toenjang* and diets high in soy content have led to *toenjang* enjoying a newfound status as a health food at present. As soybeans are high in protein, they offer an alternative protein source for those who avoid animal protein due to cholesterol concerns or the pursuit of a vegetarian diet. Other research sees *toenjang* as being an anti-carcinogen, effective in lowering high blood pressure, and as an antioxidant, among other effects. While such research is ongoing and not yet conclusive, it is clear that *toenjang* is not only an excellent seasoning, but that it is also a healthy food. Koreans in past times also recognized the curative properties of *toenjang*; the *Tong'ŭi pogam* ('Exemplar of Eastern [i.e., Korean] medicine, 1613') states that *toenjang* is good for reliving headaches and fevers, and folk medicine practices have long held that a dressing of *toenjang* was an excellent remedy for a bee-sting or minor abrasion.

Koch'ujang is the third of the three major *jang* in Korean cuisine. In general, this condiment is made by mixing *meju* powder, glutinous rice or regular boiled rice and red chilli pepper powder, and then fermenting the entire mixture. Regional variations include *koch'ujang* made with barley, wheat flour, red beans and sweet potatoes, which are then mixed with the main ingredients of soybeans and chilli pepper powder. *Koch'ujang* is a relatively new food in Korean cuisine as chilli peppers were not introduced to the peninsula until the late sixteenth century. Nonetheless, this spicy seasoning is now an important ingredient in flavouring soups, stews and vegetables.

In addition to the three *jang* described above, other seasonings are highly important in Korean cuisine. Sesame oil (*ch'am kirŭm*) and perilla oil (*tŭl kirŭm*) are the chief oils used in preparing foods, sauces and dipping sauces. Sesame oil, made by crushing sesame seeds, has a fragrant scent that accents the taste of food and is used in the preparation of meats and vegetables. Perilla oil, produced by crushing perilla seeds, is more common in the southern parts of the peninsula as perilla is not cultivated in the colder northern areas. Like sesame oil, this oil has a delicate fragrance, and is commonly used to prepare vegetable side dishes. It is also used as a dipping sauce for meats. These two oils are also used to lightly coat sheets of laver, a type of seaweed, before roasting, creating a popular and nutritious side-dish.

Fresh vegetables are also essential for seasoning in Korean cuisine. Chief among vegetables are garlic and chilli peppers, both of which are prominent in Korean foods. Garlic, although a food thought to have originated in central Asia or the Middle East, has long been cultivated on the Korean peninsula, as seen in the above-mentioned Tan'gun myth of the Kojosŏn kingdom; other records from the Three Kingdoms period demonstrate that cultivation of garlic was widespread by this time. While the garlic clove, chopped or crushed, is used for various seasonings, the stalk of the plant is also eaten as a vegetable side-dish.

Chilli peppers, though they have a relatively brief history in Korea, have become an essential component in Korean cuisine. A record from the early seventeenth century reveals that chilli peppers were introduced to Korea via Japan. This first record, written by Yi Sugwang, was hardly supportive of chilli peppers and instead informed that these were a 'great poison.' He continued that the plant had been brought from Japan, but was now commonly grown in Korea; further, he added that this spicy food was often served in drinking-houses.[23] As Yi's record was written in 1614, the introduction of chilli peppers must have occurred some years before his account, as they had already become a commonly-cultivated crop.

Notwithstanding the negative comments of Yi Sugwang, chilli peppers soon became used in many foods as a spicy seasoning, perhaps most notably *kimch'i*. The bright red colour of ripe peppers also enhanced the

This dish of stir-fried translucent noodles and vegetables (*chapch'ae*) demonstrates the idea of adding decorative garnishes to create a more visually appealing dish.

visual appeal of dishes and the long-standing belief that the colour red would help drive away baneful spirits or bad luck redoubled the popularity of chilli peppers as an ingredient in foods. Today, some four centuries after the introduction of chilli peppers to Korean cuisine, it is very difficult to imagine Korean foods without them.

A seasoning that provides flavour to foods such as *kimch'i* and is also eaten as a side-dish is *chŏtkal*, salt-fermented seafood. A very similar salt-fermented seafood is *chŏt*, which is only used for seasoning foods and not as a side-dish. These two foodstuffs are made with the flesh or innards of fish such a cod, corvine, herring, anchovies and shellfish such as shrimp. Salt is added to the seafood, and fermentation takes place when the enzymes in the seafood begins to break down the flesh. This preparation process allowed seafood to be preserved and enjoyed as a side-dish in areas distant from the sea.

Other basic seasonings used in Korean cuisine include salt, vinegar, sugar, ginger, mustard, green onion, sesame and various types of pepper. Generally when preparing a dish, several seasonings are used to create a unique flavour with different nuances of taste. Such combinations of seasonings are a characteristic of Korean foods.

Seasoning is not only a matter of taste, but also visual delight. *Komyŏng* is the term for the visual, or decorative, garnishes used in Korean cooking. Based on the Five Phases (*ohaeng*) found in the cosmology of East Asia, many Korean foods feature the five colours of blue/green, red, yellow, white and black.[24] For a green garnish, onion, squash, cucumber, or other such vegetables are shredded to add colour. For red, chilli peppers, carrots or jujubes are cut into thin strips for visual effect. Yellow and white are achieved by separating egg yolks and whites, frying very thinly and cutting into strips; black colour is provided by dark-coloured mushrooms or laver. Of course, such extravagant preparation of foods was not an everyday occurrence for people in pre-modern Korea and was mostly reserved for those in the royal palace or the uppermost status groups.

The Five Phases also relate to the five tastes of sour, bitter, sweet, spicy and salty found in Korean food. In a similar manner to the mixing of the five colours mentioned above, the blending and contrasting of tastes in food was an ideal in meal preparation. Such notions of food preparation certainly mirror the belief that food put into the body was a type of medicine and something that should be carefully managed. The proper balance of the five tastes has long been thought an important means to increase the vigour and energy of one's body.[25]

Kimch'i

As essential as rice is to a Korean meal, a table without *kimch'i* is almost unimaginable. There are literally hundreds of varieties of *kimch'i*, with new types created every day. To see the importance of *kimch'i* to Korean cuisine, we only need to look at the old saying '*kimch'i* is half of all the food provisions' (*kimch'i nŭn chŏlban yangsik*). Indeed, a meal

Yŏlmu kimch'i is made with the stems and leaves of young *yŏlmu* radish plants that are common in the summer. It has a refreshing and tangy taste.

without *kimch'i* is all but unheard of and most homes in pre-modern Korea had large stocks of *kimch'i* to ensure year-round availability.

For those unacquainted with Korean cuisine, this begs the question: what is *kimch'i*? It is, in short, a type of food that is made by salting and fermenting various vegetables such as cabbage and radishes.[26] In times before refrigeration, such vegetables were very difficult to store during the long winter months as they have a high water content. Hence, fermentation was developed as a means to preserve vegetables over long winters.

While historical records do not have a definitive date for the advent of fermented vegetables, we do know that the peoples living on and around the Korean peninsula in ancient times had mastered the process of fermenting soybeans among other items.[27] It is thought that fermentation processing was also used to preserve vegetables in early kingdoms; certainly by the Koryŏ dynasty fermented vegetables were commonplace as revealed in the following poem written by Yi Kyubo (1168–1241):

> Pickled radish slices make a good summer side-dish,
> Radish preserved in salt is a winter side-dish from start to end.
> The roots in the earth grow plumper everyday,
> Harvesting after the frost, a slice cut by a knife tastes like a pear.[28]

Records in the Chosŏn period indicate that there were some 150 varieties of *kimch'i*. Before the introduction of chilli peppers to Korea in the early seventeenth century, *kimch'i* was seasoned with ingredients such as garlic, ginger and Chinese peppercorns. A fifteenth-century writer refers to *kimch'i* as a 'golden-yellow vegetable' (*hwangje*), demonstrating a very different dish from today's *kimch'i*.[29] Chilli pepper, however, soon became a key ingredient in making *kimch'i*. Also important to the flavour of *kimch'i* are the various types of *chŏtkal*, salt-fermented seafood, that are added to vegetables as fermenting and flavouring agents.

Climatic variations and availability of different seasonings have resulted in a wide array of *kimch'i* types on the Korean peninsula. The *kimch'i* of the northern regions tends to be less spicy and salty than that of the southern areas; moreover, the main fermenting and flavour agents of the north are generally shrimp and yellow corvine *chŏt* (fermented seafood used as seasoning), whereas in the south anchovy *chŏt* is predominant. Other differences are seen in the types of vegetables used in making *kimch'i*.

Paek kimch'i is made with Chinese cabbage that is seasoned with garlic and ginger, among other spices, before a short fermentation period of two to three days. It has a crunchy and mild flavour.

In pre-modern Korea and even today in some households, *kimch'i* is prepared for the winter months in late autumn in a process known as *kimjang* (stockpiling *kimch'i*). After the autumn harvest of vegetables like radishes and Chinese cabbages, womenfolk of a particular household or village would begin preparations for making the winter *kimch'i*. As each household needed a large amount of *kimch'i* for winter provisions – about 100–150 heads of Chinese cabbage alone – the arduous work of preparation was done with other families in a reciprocal arrangement known as a *p'umasi*. This allowed necessary tasks to be done in a more efficient manner and also provided an important space for camaraderie and sharing of techniques for making tasty *kimch'i*. The *p'umasi* work-sharing system was also a common feature of laborious tasks such as transplanting rice plants and weeding rice paddies.

In preparing *kimch'i*, the cabbages are first soaked in brine for ten to twelve hours. During this period, the ingredients that will later be used to coat and season the cabbage are prepared. Common seasonings include mustard leaf, ginger, sliced radish, garlic, green onion, salt, chilli pepper powder and *chŏt*; variations include adding raw fish, oysters or shrimp, or shiitake mushrooms. After the cabbages are

washed in water and drained, the cabbage leaves are coated with the seasoning and then placed in earthenware jars for fermentation. The ideal temperature for *kimch'i* is around 5° Celsius and thus in pre-modern Korea the earthenware jars were buried to the neck in the ground to keep the *kimch'i* from either freezing or becoming too warm, either of which would ruin the taste of the *kimch'i*. The earthenware jars were further covered with rice-straw matting which not only kept out the cold, but also facilitated the reproduction of micro-organisms that helped the *kimch'i* mature. In this way, families were able to ensure that they would have a supply of vegetables throughout the winter months.

Some common types of *kimch'i* are the above described Chinese cabbage variety (*paech'u kimch'i*), *kkaktugi*, *possam kimch'i*, *p'a kimch'i* and *ch'onggak kimch'i*. *Kkaktugi* is made by cutting daikon radishes into small cubes and then salting; it is then fermented and seasoned by adding chilli pepper powder, shrimp *chŏt*, garlic, ginger and green onion, among other seasonings. *Posam kimch'i*, once reserved for the royal family, is made from salted cabbage that is cut into about four centimetre portions wrapped around various seasonings. Then the entire leaf is fermented with the seasonings. *P'a kimch'i* is made with green onions or scallions and anchovy *chŏt*, while *ch'onggak kimch'i* is made with *alta'ri* radishes that are seasoned with chilli pepper powder, garlic and ginger, among other ingredients. There are of course many variations on these basic recipes that reflect regional and personal preferences.

Kimch'i provided not only a tasty side-dish for pre-modern diets, but further is a food that is rich in vitamins A, B and C, and minerals such as calcium, potassium and iron. Moreover, the *chŏt* or raw seafood put into many types of *kimch'i* provides protein. And since *kimch'i* is fermented by lactic acid, it also aids digestion and enhances the ability of the intestines to self-clean. In all, it is a highly nutritious food.

The importance of *kimch'i* in Korean food is still recognized today, as it is probably the main food associated with Korea. There is even a *kimch'i* museum in Seoul that provides visitors with an interesting look at the history, health benefits and preparation techniques of this important dish. The museum also features a tasting room where one can sample a variety of *kimch'i* dishes.

Vegetables

> A bunch of wild parsley, unearthed and cleaned,
> Not for another, but I offer this only to you, my dearest.
> It may not be fragrant, but taste again and see.[30]

In addition to *kimch'i* there are many other herbs and vegetables that are important in Korean cuisine. Collectively known as *namul*, these can be vegetables cultivated in fields or wild herbs and plants that are gathered from the many mountains. The tradition of incorporating numerous vegetables and greens into foods probably is an ancient one that evolved from pre-agrarian times and was greatly enhanced by Buddhist beliefs that one should refrain from eating meat. Temple food is the zenith of *namul* cuisine, revealing great knowledge of the tastes of wild herbs and various cultivated vegetables. Nowadays, *namul* side-dishes provide important flavour accents to Korean cuisine and also important sources of vitamins.

Intimate knowledge of their natural surroundings, and perhaps the hardships of life for the peasantry, allowed Koreans in pre-modern times to catalogue vast knowledge of edible wild plants. A task of women and children, especially young girls, was to collect edible greens from nearby areas. There are numerous folksongs demonstrating this, such as the following stanza from a song entitled 'Tŭlnamul k'ae norae' ('Song of Picking Greens in the Field'):

Minari.

Gambolling, let's go to collect greens.
What greens shall we go gather?
In Dog Dung Field, wild parsley;
Crisply snipped off, and bring it [to],
Parboil in clear stream water,
[Then] Rinse in the water of the Han River.
For Mother, I will prepare a silver table,
For Father a gold table,
For older brother a flower table . . . [31]

In the above song we see the gathering and preparation of wild parsley (*tol minari*) and also the filial feelings associated with providing such a food to one's family. Other songs tell of digging for the roots of broad-leafed bellflowers (*toraji*) and gathering the young leaves of plantain (*chilgyŏngi*) along with collecting greens in the mountains. Such songs not only provided a means of transmitting knowledge of which greens to gather and how to prepare, but also offered a form of relief from the tedium associated with the task of searching for them.

While much of this knowledge was transmitted orally from generation to generation, it was also formally classified in the form of famine-relief books. The interest of Koreans in native plants and herbs reaches back quite far into history. *Hyang'yak kugŭp-pang* ('Emergency Folk Medicine Remedies') is a medical work published in the mid-thirteenth century and includes much information on the medicinal qualities of common herbs found in Korea. In the Chosŏn dynasty *Kuhwang ch'waryo* ('Concise Reference for Famine Relief') was first published in 1554 as a response to a poor harvest. The work lists some 851 types of edible plants and herbs, well demonstrating the depth of understanding of the natural environment. Among the information in this work are recipes for making porridge from pine needles and for making flour from the bark of the elm tree. While such foods were clearly for dire times, the classification and diffusion of this information certainly helped the everyday lives of the people in regards to possible foodstuffs. Subsequent to these works, there were numerous publications during the Chosŏn dynasty that expanded and augmented knowledge of nature.

In general, *namul* are classified based upon preparation method: *sukch'ae*, *saengcha'e* and *chapch'ae*. *Sukch'ae*, meaning cooked vegetables, can be further divided into two sub-categories depending on cooking method. First are those vegetables that are served after parboiling and seasoning. After parboiling vegetables, they are then drained and lightly seasoned with condiments such as salt, *kanjang*, *koch'ujang*, garlic, chilli pepper powder and sesame oil. The other category is those vegetables that are cooked in a pan with a small amount

Various vegetables can be served as *ssam*. In this photo we can see red leaf lettuce, Chinese cabbage (both fresh and fermented) and laver, among others. *Ssam* is commonly served with chilli peppers and *toenjang*.

of oil. Preparation depends on the vegetable with spinach, bean sprouts and artemisia being parboiled, and fernbrake, eggplant, mushrooms and bellflower being stir-fried.

Saengch'ae, or raw vegetables, are *namul* that are prepared and eaten without cooking. Raw vegetables have long been a part of Korean cuisine as seen in an eighteenth-century literary miscellany stating, 'The taste of Koryŏ *saengch'ae* is very good and the mountains are fraught with the scent of mushrooms. The people wrap rice in vegetables and then eat it.'[32] The food that is described in this account is known as *ssam* and is still a popular food today. At the beginning of this chapter is a stanza from the poem 'Ŏbu sasi sa' ('The Angler's Calendar', 1651) written by Yun Sŏndo (1587–1675), one of the foremost poets of the Chosŏn period, that tells of wrapping rice in lotus leaves. More common vegetables used to wrap rice are lettuce and *ssukkat* (crown daisy leaves) in the summer and steamed pumpkin leaves in the autumn, among others. Rice is put into the leaf and then a seasoning such as *koch'ujang* or *toenjang* is added before wrapping the leaf up and eating.

Other *saengch'ae* are seasoned and then eaten. The condiments for seasoning these vegetables are quite similar to those mentioned above, and by not cooking the *namul*, a stronger taste is preserved. Other times vinegar is used to accent a crisp taste. Vegetables served in this manner include *tŏdŏk* (an edible root), cucumbers and radishes.

Pŏsŏt pokkŭm is a dish of stir-fried mushrooms lightly seasoned with sesame oil and black pepper.

Samsaek namul. This instance has, clockwise from the top, bracken, bean sprouts and spinach.

The final manner of preparation is the *chapch'ae* vegetables, or those that are fried with meat. In general several types of vegetables are mixed together and then stir-fried with the meat. A common variation of this dish further adds translucent noodles to the vegetables and meat, a dish known by the same name, *chapch'ae*.

Although there are various means of serving *namul*, it is a practice in Korean cuisine to place three or more types of *namul* in a single dish. This allows both diversity in tastes and a good visual image when the *namul* are coordinated for contrast. For example, in the winter *kobi* (royal fern), *toraji* (bellflower roots) and spinach present an excellent visual presentation of brown, beige and deep green, along with quite different textures and tastes. Such preparation is known as 'three-colour' *namul* and there are numerous variations for different seasons and regions. Even more elaborate are the 'five-colour' *namul* that combine five contrasting vegetables.

Soups

Meals in Korea inevitably include a soup or stew along with rice, side-dishes and *kimch'i*. Different from some Western or Chinese traditions where soup is served at either the beginning or end of the main course, in Korean cuisine it is served as a part of the main meal. Soups, known as *kuk* in Korean, can be made with ingredients such as meats, shellfish and vegetables. A more formal word for soups is *t'ang*, and these soups are generally prepared with meats and to be offered at ancestral rites. Stews, known as *tchigae*, are thicker than simple soups and are also a common element in meals.

In general, soups can be divided into four broad categories depending upon ingredients and the main condiments used for seasoning. Clear soups (*malgŭn kuk*) are flavoured with *kanjang*. If meat is used in these soups, a small amount is boiled for a long period of time. Other soups use seafood, either fresh or dried, and still others use only vegetables. Common varieties of these soups include *miyŏk kuk* made from brown seaweed, *mu kuk* (daikon radish soup) and *pugŏ kuk*, made with dried Pollack. *Miyŏk kuk* is particularly prominent in Korea cuisine as a food eaten on one's birthday, and is also taken by women after childbirth.

Soups flavoured chiefly with *toenjang* comprise the second classification of soups and are known as *t'ojang kuk*. Oftentimes, seafood such as clams, dried anchovies or shrimp are added to these soups to create a rich stock with which other ingredients are mixed. *Koch'ujang* is also commonly included to make the soup spicier. Different soups of

Kalbi t'ang, beef-rib soup garnished with spring onions, whole garlic and egg strips. Other variations of this popular dish call for adding jujubes, ginseng or chestnuts.

this variation include *naeng'i kuk* (shepherd's purse soup), *paech'u soktae kuk* (Chinese cabbage-heart soup), and *minŏ maeun t'ang* (spicy croaker soup).

Soups made by boiling cattle bones or cartilage are known as *kom kuk*. In these soups, various cow bones such as tail-bones, leg-bones and rib-bones are boiled for long periods of times to extract the fat, marrow and potassium, eventually resulting in a milky-white soup. Bones can be boiled with good amounts of meat still attached, or nearly bare. Other varieties of *kom kuk* use other parts of cattle including the head and intestines. Commonly, the only seasoning used is salt. These soups, while widely enjoyed today, are largely foods developed by peasants in pre-modern Korea as ways to fully utilize all parts of a cow. There are many types of these soups including *kkori kom t'ang* (oxtail soup), *kalbi t'ang* (beef rib soup), and *sŏllŏng t'ang* (beef bone soup).

The final classification for soups is that of *naeng kuk*, or cold soups, that are now usually eaten during the hot summer months. Common varieties of these soups include that made with seaweed (*miyŏk naeng kuk*) or cucumbers *(oi naeng kuk)*. The seasoning of these soups is generally light, consisting of *kanjang* and sometimes a small amount of sesame oil. Another type of cold soup is roasted chicken and sesame soup (*imja sut'ang*). In this soup, boiled, shredded chicken is mixed with cucumbers, shiitake mushrooms and ginger, among other vegetables. These ingredients are then added to a cold chicken broth that has been prepared with ground white sesame (*imja*). This soup was a popular dish enjoyed at the royal palace in the summer months.

The thicker pot stews known as *tchigae* are served most often as a shared side-dish rather than in individual bowls as the soups discussed above are. In general, *tchigae* are cooked and served in the same vessel, a glazed earthenware pot (*ttukpaegi*). Compared to a regular metal cooking pot, the earthenware pot retains heat much better and allows the stew to continue cooking after it has been removed from the heat source.

One of the most common of the *tchigae* is that made with soybean paste. *Toenjang tchigae*, while having many variations, was made throughout the Korean peninsula in past times, and remains a staple in Korean homes today. *Toenjang* is added to water and boiled with various vegetables, marine products, and often tofu, resulting in a thick and hearty stew to complement rice and side dishes. The combination of this stew varied with season, availability of ingredients and personal preference, and thus well represents the diverse nature

Toenjang tchigae is a staple not only in Korean restaurants but also in homes.

Ch'uŏt'ang is a thick soup made with loach fish, vegetables, sesame, *toenjang* and *koch'u-jang* paste.

of Korean cuisine, which has widely varied styles of preparing the same foods.

Tchigae made with sour *kimch'i* are also common and combine *kimch'i* with tofu and sometimes pork for additional flavour. Other *tchigae* include those seasoned primarily with *koch'ujang* and featuring various marine products (*koch'ujang tchigae*), *maeun t'ang*, a popular *tchigae* of the south that combines fish and vegetables in a spicy soup seasoned with either *koch'ujang* or chilli pepper powder and a stew seasoned with tiny salted shrimp (*saeujŏt tchigae*). There are numerous other *tchigae* that are simply put together with whatever ingredients are on hand.

Meats and Fish

> There was a country fellow surnamed Kim with a large and fat mid-section who very much enjoyed eating. He particularly liked steamed carp casserole [*pungŏ tchim*]. His method for cooking this began with making a long, slender underground flue of several ten lengths at which end he installed a cast iron cooking pot (sot). At the other end he made a fire hole in which he loaded charcoal and wood, slowly allowing the heat to reach the cooking pot at the other end. [To the pot] he added sesame oil, sweetened soy sauce, good vinegar, ginger, black pepper, green onions, chives and so on, cooking until tender. After putting a big carp in the pot, he cooked the whole stew overnight until it was well done. The taste was exquisitely beautiful.[33]

While meats in pre-modern Korea were much less common than today, they were still important and enjoyed, as seen in the above fifteenth-century account of preparing steamed carp. Certainly since the time of the first inhabitants of the Korean peninsula, various meats and seafood have been integral elements in diets. In ancient times, meat was obtained either through hunting or fishing, whereas even before the time of the Three Kingdoms, livestock was raised on a small scale. Meats could be roasted or added to soups and stews, depending on the type and quantity of meat available. Economic status and proximity to the sea also dictated the amount of meat or fish in an individual's diet.

Of all the meats in Korean cuisine, it is beef that perhaps holds the highest position. This is not to state, however, that beef was consumed to a greater degree than fish or pork in past times, as it was not. Yet the value of cattle as not only a source of food but also as a work animal cannot be overlooked. In fact, in past times cattle were regarded as *saenggu*, servants who assisted with livelihood of a family in the same way as human servants or retainers. Cows were further honoured on the first 'cow' day of the lunar New Year, and given the day off and special feed.[34] While such an honour might have been lost on the cattle, the fact that a day was set aside for the animals bespeaks the importance of the cow to a family's well-being.

Given the amount of space and feed needed to raise large numbers of livestock, cattle-rearing was not practiced on a major scale in most of Korean history. Nonetheless, beef was incorporated into Korean cuisine from an early time. Historical records indicate that cattle were

Kalbi grilled over charcoal.

domesticated by at least the first century CE and that by the Three King-doms period, cattle were indispensable both in farming and as a source of food. In the Buddhist Koryŏ dynasty, the slaughter of cattle for food was prohibited, but after the late thirteenth-century invasion by the Mongols eating beef became more widespread. In the subsequent Chosŏn dynasty, cattle rearing was encouraged by the government as it increased both the number and quality of the animals. A seventeenth-century writer wrote that of all foods, 'beef is the most beneficial to humans.'[35]

While there are many beef dishes in Korean cuisine at present, one should be cognizant that in past times beef was not a daily dish for most Koreans. Rather, it was a food to be enjoyed on special occasions or by those in the very uppermost social or economic groups. The present-day commonness of beef dishes is very much a phenomenon of the last decades of the twentieth century.

Beef is prepared in various ways such as roasting, boiling in soups or drying. Common dishes include beef roasted over charcoal, such as *kalbi* (beef ribs) or *tŭngsim* (thinly sliced rib-eye). In the case of *kalbi*, seasonings such as sesame oil, garlic and *kanjang* are used to enhance the flavour of the meat, whereas *tŭngsim* is cooked without seasoning and then lightly dipped into a mixture of sesame oil and salt directly before eating. The popular dish *pulgogi* is thinly sliced beef marinated in *kanjang*, honey, chopped green onions, sesame seeds and black pepper and then grilled over charcoal.

Beef is also utilized in soups and stews such as the *kkori kom t'ang* (oxtail soup) and *kalbi t'ang* (beef rib soup) mentioned above. Many other soups use beef bones for stock, thus fully utilizing all parts of the cow. Beef is also thinly sliced and dried into jerky (*yukp'o*) as a means of preserving the meat for long periods of time. Dried and cooked beef are also used in the preparation of various side dishes to enhance the flavour of vegetables and herbs.

Like cattle rearing, the raising of hogs for meat has long been practiced on the Korean peninsula. Based on Chinese historical records, we can understand that early peoples on and around the Korean peninsula have been raising pigs for at least two millennia. Pigs were most often raised in pens on the peninsula, but on Cheju Island they were raised in special pens built around raised privies, and thus consumed human excrement. The meat from such pigs, known as *ttong twaeji* (dung hogs) was highly prized and is still considered an Island delicacy.

Pork is prepared and eaten in various ways, with roasting and adding to stews most common. Roasted pork belly (*samgyŏp sal*) is a favourite, and pork is often added to stews such as *kimch'i tchigae*. Interestingly, there were many foods that were avoided when eating pork such as bell-flower (*toraji*) and lotus root (*yŏn ppuri*), which were thought to cause diarrhoea in conjunction with pork. On the other hand, certain parts of pigs were thought to have medicinal or curative power. For example the

Samkyŏp sal cooked on an earthenware pan along with garlic. The egg in the centre is a speciality of this particular restaurant. Other popular methods of cooking include on thin stone slabs or on a grill over charcoal.

blood taken from the tail of a pig was believed to have the power to revive a person who had suddenly collapsed and died.

Aside from combinations to be avoided or medicinal attributes of hogs, pork was enjoyed as a relatively common meat in pre-modern times. Nearly all parts of the pig were utilized in various dishes, such as roasted pork dishes using the ribs (*twaeji kalbi*), dishes using steamed or smoked pork, and stews and soups. Pork skin was also roasted and eaten as a side-dish.

Chicken is another important meat for both pre-modern and modern Korea. The raising of chickens seems to have been widespread by the time of the Silla kingdom as a legend concerning Kim Alji (65–?), the founder of the Kyŏngju Kim family. The legend tells that his appearance in the forest as an infant was announced by the cry of a white chicken.[36] The auspicious birth of a clan's founder could have only been divulged by an animal with preternatural qualities, and this bespeaks of the importance of the chicken to the well-being of people in this age.

The position of chicken in Korean cuisine comes only after that of beef and pork, and it is served in a variety of ways including roasting, steamed with vegetables and in soups. Eggs, of course, are important in numerous dishes or alone, and nearly all parts of the chicken are eaten including the gizzard, liver and feet. Whole young fryers are used in the seasonal summer dish *samgye t'ang* (chicken and ginseng soup) which is believed an important means to combat effects of summer heat. *Taktchim* (steamed chicken with vegetables) is chicken simmered along with various vegetables in a spicy sauce, and roasted chicken feet were traditionally eaten as a side-dish when drinking wine.

Dogs are also raised for meat and are a prominent summer dish. The meat is eaten either roasted or in soups, and is said to be an excellent general panacea for overall health. Particularly, dog is eaten in the summer as the spicy soup is believed to help provide strength to the body to combat the hot and humid summer months. The taking of spicy hot soups in the summer is believed a means to ensure good health by balancing the temperature of one's *ki* (vital energy of the body) with that of the environment. Other meats in pre-modern diets included wild animals such as pheasant and deer, and sheep or goat which generally was taken as medicine.

Both freshwater and saltwater fish were ubiquitous in Korean cuisine in past times. Fish can be eaten raw, broiled, dried, or added to soups, stews and side dishes; indeed, there is rarely a meal served without

A scene from an open-air market. The sign-boards at the front of the picture are advertising dog meat.

some sort of marine product present. This, of course, reflects the fact that Korea is a peninsula bordered by rich waters that offer a bounty of marine creatures.

An account from the early twelfth century by a Song Chinese (960–1279) traveller to Koryŏ discloses that although there were numerous sheep and hogs present, these were largely reserved for those of the upper status groups. Commoners, on the other hand, ate much seafood such as shrimp, clams, oysters, abalone, and loach among other seafood.[37] The reason for this distinction seems to have been one of economics, according to this writer. Fish were readily available to those living in coastal areas.

Grilled fish has long been part of the diets in Korea. Some fish served in such a fashion include mackerel, hairtail, croaker and Pacific herring, among many others. The fish is commonly lightly sprinkled with salt and then either cooked whole or as a fillet. The fish is then eaten as a side-dish along with rice. Dried fish is also common. Naturally, drying the fish allowed for easier storage and permitted transportation to areas distant from the coastal regions. Favourites for drying include the yellow corvina and croaker, both of which are preserved in salt and dried whole. Thus preserved, the fish were easily brought to inland markets for sale in past days. For cooking, the fish is fried in a small amount of oil and served as a side-dish. Anchovies are another fish that are dried as a means of preservation and are used as stock for some soups and also as a side-dish, either alone or mixed with vegetables.

Seasoned saltwater eel grilled over charcoal.

Salmon *hoe.*

For those living nearby the coast, raw fish (*hoe*) was a popular dish. Served either as a complement to a meal or as a side-dish for drinking spirits, raw fish was thinly sliced and then dipped in *koch'ujang* or *kanjang* directly before eating. Many varieties of fish were eaten this way along with octopus, squid, sea cucumber, shellfish and other marine products. Raw fish was also mixed with rice and vegetables or served in cold soups.

There were many ways to prepare and enjoy fish as seen in the following stanza of 'Hwansan pyŏlgok' ('Song of Return to the Mountain'), a poem attributed to the famous Confucian scholar Yi Hwang (1501-1570):

The single ribbon of pure water
Is the same colour as the vast heavens.
In the thin white threads of the net

Cast into the shallows,
Silver-scaled jade measuring sticks
Are caught here and there.
I gather them all
Big and little,
The little ones I boil
And the big ones I slice [and eat] raw.
Wine from an earthenware pot
I pour into an unadorned cup,
Drinking and persuading others to do the same,
I drink until after I am drunk.
When the sun sinks into the waters
And the moon rises over the eastern hill,
Stumbling and weaving
I return to my brushwood gate.
My son helps me in my drunkenness
And my slender wife welcomes me.
I then dare to think that I alone am
The master of the rivers and mountains.[38]

Fish of all sorts would have been readily available and relatively easy to obtain for most Koreans in past times. While the above account is somewhat idealized in that it was composed by an upper-status scholar who was fishing for pleasure rather than out of necessity, we can feel in Yi's words the simple pleasures of fishing, eating and drinking.

Shellfish such as clams, oysters and abalone were also common. Oftentimes these shellfish were used in soups as stock. A recipe for clams in a sixteenth-century literary miscellany tells of boiling clams with lard and wine – wine, asserts this writer, is necessary to remove the 'fishy' taste and should be used in cooking all seafood.[39] Other uses include mixing raw oysters into Chinese cabbage *kimch'i*, both for flavouring and to extend the life of the vegetable, mixing raw oysters or clams into rice before cooking and making a thick rice porridge with bits of abalone – a special dish of southern coastal areas known as *chŏnbok chuk*. Shrimp of all sizes are also prominent and have a wide range of uses, from a salty seasoning (*seau chŏt*) used for making some types of *kimch'i*, to grilling whole large shrimp or drying them and then mixing with vegetables as a side-dish.

This dish is a combination of chilli peppers and dried anchovies. The combination of crunchy and soft textures provides excellent contrast.

Other marine products important to Korean diets include squid, cuttlefish and octopus. Squid, in particular, was a common catch and used in soups and side-dishes, or dried and eaten as a side-dish with spirits. Another common use for these meats was to cook with vegetables in a spicy stew. Shredded and seasoned cuttlefish is a popular snack, while raw small octopus cut and dipped in *koch'ujang* before eating is an excellent side-dish for drinking spirits.

Such daily foods as described in this chapter would have varied greatly in pre-modern times depending upon one's locale and economic means. While the ideal of boiled rice served with a variety of side-dishes was one that perhaps all people sought, in reality such fare would have been enjoyed mostly by those of the uppermost economic and social status groups. The development of dishes such as rice, or other grains, mixed with vegetables (*pibim pap*) came from peasant households attempting to make their meagre resources into more palatable foods. The popularity of dishes like this today, however, demonstrates that the art of cooking was not by any means confined to the upper-status groups.

This side-dish features seasoned dried squid and chives.

Puch'u much'im is a side-dish of uncooked chives mixed with *koch'ujang* paste and sesame seeds.

2 Ritual and Seasonal Foods

> The women of the next house compete riding the swing,
> Bound to the rope in midair, they swing and play like heavenly
> fairies.
> As the wind pushes the coloured ropes towards the heavens,
> The sound of their ornaments chimes amidst the willows.
> Hŏ Nansŏrhŏn (1563–1589)[1]

Various times of the year are highlighted by festivities that allow us to come together and collectively celebrate and enjoy life. Pre-modern Korea was no different in this regard, as certain commemorative dates and events were marked with ceremony and ritual. Along with folk games such as the swing-contest described in the above poem, food and drink were prominent in these events.

Ritual foods are the foods prepared for special occasions or the performance of rites. These foods can be quite distinct from the everyday fare discussed above and carry deep cultural significance and symbolic meanings. While some of these foods were enjoyed on seasonal holidays such as the lunar New Year, Harvest Festival or winter solstice, others were commonly served on felicitous occasions including birthdays or weddings. Still others were used when offering the very important ancestor rites that marked the most solemn events in the Confucian society of the Chosŏn dynasty.

There is a significant amount of crossover between some of the foods discussed in this chapter and those daily foods described in chapter One. However, the focus here will be the ritual use of food and the symbolic significance that these foods carried in a ritual context.

A mid-sixteenth-century painting depicting a seventieth birthday celebration for a high-ranking civil official entitled *Hojo nanggwan kyehoe-do* (Painting of the Celebration for the Minister of the Board of Taxation).

Historical documents demonstrate that various rites and celebratory events have been observed since the earliest recorded polities located on or around the Korean peninsula. Mass celebrations are noted in nearly all these ancient kingdoms such as the Yŏnggo (spirit-invoking drums) of Puyŏ (*c.* 1st century BCE–3rd century CE) or the Tongmaeng (a harvest festival to the founder) of Koguryŏ (BCE 37–668 CE). Early

Men and children eating
at an inn in the late
Chosŏn period.

Chinese histories of the region uniformly note the propensity of these ancient peoples for marking celebratory festivals with song, dance, food and drink.[2] We can understand the importance of food in these ceremonies as being reflective of the bond between the supernatural and the survival of the people, particularly in regards to agriculture. Thus, these ancient ceremonies were rituals conducted as a means to thank the forces governing agriculture for the present harvest and to petition for future abundance. The relevance of these ceremonies to the survival of the people, and by extension the kingdom, can be seen in the participation of all members of the society in the rites, even to the extent of releasing prisoners to join in the thanks.

The amalgamation of religious worship, social interaction and cuisine is prominent in the rites of pre-modern Korea and such a bond continues till the present day. Included here are those foods that are attributed certain medicinal qualities or are thought to be conducive to bettering one's health. The present heightened awareness of the importance of good dietary habits in contemporary Korea has created even more interest in traditional foods thought to have curative or preventive properties. Yet, this awareness has long been acknowledged in Korea. The early seventeenth-century *Tongŭi pogam* ('Exemplar of Eastern [i.e., Korean] Medicine') clearly demonstrates this: 'Food is exactly medicine; since eating food correctly is tantamount to the function of medicine, if illness occurs one must first regulate his diet and then take medicine.'³

Birthday Celebrations

Directly after the birth of a child, a new mother is given special foods which are believed to be particularly beneficial to her. Most notable is *miyŏk-kuk*, a soup made by cooking brown kelp, a type of seaweed, in a clam stock. This clear soup is high in protein and also easy to digest, making it an ideal food for the woman who has just undergone the physical exertion associated with childbirth.

The soup is all the more important for its role in offering thanks to the deity believed to govern childbirth in Korean folk customs. Folk beliefs inform that the Samsin Grandmother was charged by the Jade Emperor with regulating the number of children in this world and assisting with childbirth. Accordingly, a table with bowls of cooked white rice and *miyŏk-kuk* is offered as thanks to this deity on the third and seventh days after childbirth; after the short ritual the new mother is then served the food. An interesting anecdote concerning childbirth and the Samsin Grandmother purports to explain the bluish birthmark on the buttocks of all Korean children (this mark generally disappears

Miyŏk-kuk.

by the second birthday). Folklore holds that this mark is the result of a slap by the Samsin Grandmother to hurry the baby into this world, showing the importance of this deity.

While *miyŏk-kuk* is acknowledged as being excellent for pregnant women and new mothers, there were other foods that were to be avoided by women when pregnant in past times. Duck in any form was taboo for pregnant women as folk beliefs held that if an expectant mother were to eat it, her baby would waddle like a duck when walking. A perhaps more plausible prohibition was on boneless marine creatures like octopus, squid and cuttlefish, since the small bones of fish were seen as being good for an expectant mother; modern science supports this notion somewhat, as we now know that the small bones in fish are a good source of calcium, an important nutrient for women. Finally, *sujŏnggwa*, a tea made from cinnamon and persimmons, was to be avoided by pregnant women as it was believed that the spicy cinnamon would lead to the baby being overheated and cause it to suffer from congenital fever.

In pre-modern times the one-hundredth-day anniversary of a baby's birth was marked with a celebration. For the first few months of a newborn baby's life, great care was taken to protect the child from outside contact and also to allow the mother to regain her health. The one-hundredth-day celebration, known as *paegil*, was the end of this period of eschewal and marked by festivities including special foods.

The morning of *paegil* began with an offering of *miyŏk-kuk* and cooked white rice to the Samsin Grandmother; after the short rite, the foods were then eaten by the mother of the baby. Other special foods eaten on this day are mostly various types of confections, including steamed rice cakes (*paeksŏlgi*), cakes made with millet flour and red beans (*susu p'at ttŏk*), rice cake made from glutinous rice (*injŏlmi*) and filled-rice cakes steamed on pine needles (*songp'yŏn*). Each of these foods carries a special meaning in this ritual. The *paeksŏlgi* convey a wish for longevity and represent purity and sincerity. The *susu p'at ttŏk* are filled with red bean paste; the colour red has long been held effective in driving away baneful spirits in Korean folk customs and thus this food is served at the ceremony as a means to keep harmful spirits – thought to cause sickness in past times – away from the infant. *Injŏlmi* represent strength and resolution, while the five-coloured *songp'yŏn* convey the desire for the infant to grow into a person that has a balance of each of the Five Phases (*ohaeng*).

Paegsŏlgi.

In theory, the confections of the *paegil* ceremony were to be shared with one hundred houses and spread the good fortune arising from this felicitous event. By sharing these special foods throughout the community, the family of the baby announced that the child had reached this milestone and also entreated neighbors to assist with the growth of the child in future years. As such this was the first step for the child into larger society and accordingly treated with importance.

The next step in a baby's life was his or her first birthday celebration. The foods for this event are very similar to those for the *paegil*, and carry similar cultural significance. An interesting part of the first birthday celebration, known as *tol*, is a ceremony where various articles are placed in front of the baby and he or she is encouraged to grab one. Whatever article the baby grabs is believed to divine the future: taking thread equates to longevity, an arrow predicts a future in the military, a writing brush or book foretells of a scholar, rice forecasts the child becoming wealthy, the knife divines excellent skill in preparing food and jujubes prognosticate that the child's descendants will flourish. Like the *paegil* above, the child's first birthday celebration was an event that combined special foods with cultural significance and helped set the child on the path to entering society.

While a child's first ten or so birthdays largely featured the same foods as discussed above, birthday celebrations for adults had a different appearance. These celebrations generally began with a morning meal shared by adult family members. Birthday meals featured a greater number and variety of side-dishes than ordinary times as a way of marking the day. For lunch, the menu would invariably feature a noodle dish, as noodles signified a wish for long life. While the first two meals of the day

Siru ttŏk.

were mainly shared with family members, dinner was a larger feast joined by well-wishing neighbours and acquaintances. Even grander birthday feasts were prepared for sixtieth and seventieth birthday celebrations to match the importance of these days.

Modern day birthdays for children and adults alike share many of the practices described above for Chosŏn period celebrations. The special foods that were used in past times to mark these milestones are still seen in the birthday festivities of the present time, demonstrating the important bond between certain foods and customs.

Marriage Celebrations

> From the heavens are bestowed longevity and good fortune,
> And the magpie tells of never-ending blessings of prosperity.
> Having many fertile fields is not my wish,
> Rather, I yearn to spend a blissful lifetime with my love.[4]

In pre-modern Korea, marriage was much more than the bond between a man and woman. Rather, these unions represented the joining of two families and as such carried significant political, social, and economic import. This was all the more true for those of the upper-status groups, as a marriage was a means to increase the political or economic well-being of a family. Marriages were class endogamic in Chosŏn, especially for those of the upper-status groups, and these ceremonies were steeped in layers of decorum and ritual, the completion of which could take years from beginning to end. While marriage rites for lower-status groups were simpler, they still shared many of the same steps. Food, quite naturally, played an important part in marriage rites.

One of the first steps in a marriage, after all the particulars had been decided, was the sending of a wedding chest to the bride's home by the family of the bridegroom. This chest would be brought by a party of bearers, generally in the evening, and contain red and blue silk cloth along with the marriage document. It was the custom in various regions to include other items in the chest, such as chilli peppers, which signified a wish for many sons. After receiving the chest, the bride's family brought out a rice cake made in a large earthenware steamer known as a *siru*. The *siru ttŏk* was uncut and had two layers of red beans, one each for the bride and the groom, and symbolic of conjugal harmony. Additionally, the red colour of the beans was believed to ward off any baneful influences.

The marriage ceremony proper, known as the *taerye*, also featured food significantly. For an upper-status family, this would have been an extravagant event, with copious amounts of food served to relatives and neighbours. Even for a lower-status family, weddings were of no small import and the foods served to neighbours and relatives were a substantial expense for the family. The actual 'marriage' took place with the exchange of wine cups by the bride and groom. The bride offered her bridegroom two cups of wine and he offered her a single cup. This exchange was repeated before the couple shared sips of wine from a single cup, then pouring the remainder into gourds adorned with red and blue threads. This exchange and sharing of wine symbolized the new social relations of the couple and also reciprocity in their future relationship.

Another step in marriage ceremonies where food played a central role is at the bride's first meeting with her in-laws at their home after the conclusion of the actual marriage rites. This meeting, which is in reality her formal induction into her husband's home, is known as *p'ye-baek*. The bride prepared in advance at her natal home foods for this event including jujubes, chestnuts, fruit, dried beef and spirits. While the foods prepared by the new bride for her in-laws varied according to region and family tastes, some foods such as the jujubes were consistent and central to the ritual meaning of this event. Jujubes were symbolic of the bride's determination to give her in-laws an abundance of grandsons and were offered to her father-in-law. Jujubes were also considered a special 'food of heavenly fairies' and thus included in this ritual, and many others, as a petition for longevity for those who ate the fruit. This hope for future happiness was shared with the young women of the house also, who, after receiving the bows of the new bride, took the jujubes and chestnuts as a means of wishing for good luck. Spirits were frequently served at the *p'yebaek* of commoner families, but not so prominent at the same rites in upper-status families.

The actual wedding meal that the bride and groom took together varied significantly depending upon social status, geographic location, economic means and period, so generalizations are difficult. There are, however, numerous texts from the Chosŏn period that explain the details of marriage rituals and these allow an understanding of the foods served to the new couple on their wedding day. The following description of upper-status group wedding procedures is from a work compiled by the renowned scholar Chŏng Yagyong (1762–1836):

> Two tables are set up, one each for the bride and groom. The contents of each table are identical and feature nine dishes: *ttŏk*, *sikhye* (a cold, fermented rice drink), a chicken dish, a pork dish, broiled fish, soup, *kimch'i*, *jang* and white rice. The bridegroom sits to the west, the bride to the east, to the north is water, and to the south *ch'ŏngju* [clear, strained rice wine]. Before eating, both the bride and the groom take a spoonful of rice and put this in a special dish and then set it aside. Known as *kosure*, this offering is to the sundry spirits and ghosts that might be present at this ceremony and could cause bad luck if not satiated. After making this offering, the new couple then eats this meal together.[5]

Major Celebrations

In pre-modern Korea major celebrations were marked by the preparation of a feast known as a 'large table' (*k'ŭn sang*). These events include marriage ceremonies and sixtieth or seventieth birthday celebrations along with other festive occasions. Generally, any one person would in the course of their life have two to four such fêtes on their behalf. Since

Chapch'ae.

Cooked beef coated
in glutinous rice flour.

these events marked very important occasions such as giving thanks for
a long life or celebrating the bond between families in a marriage, the
atmosphere of these celebrations was not festive, but rather a mood of
deep reverence. At these time tables were piled high with beautifully
arranged and coordinated foods – more than one could ever hope to eat
– and thus reflected a wish for prosperity and good fortune for the honoree of the celebration. The table presented as such is known also as a
'wish' table (*mang sang*).

The arrangement of the large table is an important aspect of these
events and is designed to be both colourful and plentiful. The stacks of
food, especially the confections and the *ttŏk*, are arranged in 30–50-cm-
high cylindrical shapes, often with regular patterns of different colours,
creating a stunning visual effect. At other times, the difference in
colour is utilized to 'write' on the stacks of food, spelling out auspicious

Sino-Korean characters such as 'longevity' or 'fortune'. The row at the front of the table has stacks of fresh fruits, nuts and confections made with honey and oil. The next row has stacks of *ttŏk*, dried meats and fish and fried or grilled meats and fish. Closest to the seats of the honoree and his or her spouse are side-dishes such as *kimch'i*, *chapch'ae* (vegetables stir-fried with noodles), and hot beef soup with noodles (*kuksujangguk*).

These foods had numerous cultural meanings. The abundance and varieties of the foods served for these occasions are aimed at fostering goodwill among those who partake in the foods and acknowledging reciprocity between the honoree and the guests. As in the birthday and marriage celebrations mentioned earlier, holding a large feast is not only made to honour an individual milestone, but also to build upon communal harmony and acknowledge social relations. A major feast, then, helps bring together a given community and creates a space where people of various stations in life can come together in celebration.

Other cultural meanings are found in the foods served at these events. The noodle dish, as mentioned earlier, represents a wish for the longevity and health of the honoree, while the various *ttŏk* symbolize various attributes such as the desire for strength, health, longevity and prosperity.

The food prepared for ancestor rites (*cherye*) is very close to that used for other important occasions such as birthdays and weddings. Ancestor rites were conducted in pre-modern Korea several times yearly by upper-status families, and less frequently by those of lower status. The rites were a representation of the respect for the deceased and also an acknowledgement of the importance of one's ancestors. These were solemn rituals and held with great seriousness.

Placement of foods is strict and is based in part on notions found in the Five Phases and balance of *yin* and *yang*. Thus diagrams for the setting of tables have long been important for families in carrying out these rites. In general, the first row of the table holds fruit offerings with red-coloured fruits placed to the east and white-coloured ones to the west. The rows behind the fruit included dried meat, fish, *kimch'i* and various vegetable side-dishes. These foods were placed according to rules of fish to the east and meats to the west (*ŏ-dong yuk-sŏ*), root vegetables to the east and leafy vegetables to the west (*kŭn-dong yŏp-sŏ*). Also included on the table were rice, soups and wines.

The foods and wines are ceremonially offered to the ancestors in several stages. After all of the foods were presented, the ritual participants then ate the foods. The offering of food to the spirits of the deceased demonstrates the importance of food and sharing meals in Korean culture. Only the best foods are used in these rites and this reveals the depth of practices associated with filial piety in pre-modern Korean culture. Many families in contemporary Korea still conduct ancestor rites on major holidays and on the anniversary of the death of one's father or mother. The rites are very much streamlined when compared to the past, but the same emphasis on sincerity and respect for one's ancestors characterizes these events as in past times.

Not all rites in pre-modern Korea were Confucian, as shamanic and Buddhist worldviews also thrived. Shamanic rites provide an interesting contrast to the Confucian rituals. While there is some overlap in the types of food used, the underlying meanings differ. Whereas Confucian rites are held to demonstrate filial loyalty and respect for one's ancestors, shamanic rites tend to centre on the problems that humans experience in this world, such as discord, misfortune and illness. Rites are conducted to rectify these problems and help either individuals or communities heal and thrive.

Descriptions for the contents of shamanic food offerings in pre-modern Korea are very difficult to uncover, except that many

Ttŏkkuk with *mandu* dumplings.

Confucian scholars criticized this worldview as being ruinous to families, especially women, and wasteful of resources. Such criticism dates back at least to the Koryŏ period.[6] Contemporary instruction manuals for shamans describe tables set with *ttŏk*, fruit, confections and spirits much like what we can see in ancestor rites.[7] A major difference, however, are the offerings of whole pigs or cow heads. In the past, these were important parts of the payment to a shaman for performing a ritual and also symbolic of a plentiful offering to the deities being petitioned for assistance.

Seasonal Foods

> While looking around the marketplace,
>   do not forget what we need to buy;
> Buy a string of dried Pollack or a small croaker,
>   so we can greet the Harvest Moon Festival.
> Wine brewed with newly harvested rice, *sŏngp'yŏn* made of new rice,
> Tender pumpkin leaves, and clear soybean soup with taro leaves;
> These we will offer at the family graves and then share with our
>   neighbours.[8]

Closely related to ritual foods are foods prepared as seasonal dishes. These can be used to mark certain holidays such as the Harvest Moon Festival (*Ch'usŏk*) described in the above song. Moreover, these are dishes enjoyed when either certain ingredients are available or as healthy foods during particular times of the year. As such, there is significant cultural meaning attached to these foods.

Nearly every holiday in Korea is marked by a special dish or two that not only carries some import, but also adds to the festive nature of the holiday. For example, the Lunar New Year could hardly be considered complete by most Koreans without having a bowl of *ttŏkkuk*, a soup made with thinly sliced ovals of rice cake, on the morning of the New Year. This particular dish is so closely bonded with the advent of the New Year – a time when Koreans traditionally would add a year to their age – that elders often ask children how old they are by asking how many bowls of *ttŏkkuk* they have eaten. The import of this dish runs even deeper, as the bowl of soup marks the passing of the old year and the revitalization of all things in the universe, a sentiment found in the ancient religious practices of the Korean people.

In past times, *ttŏkkuk* was ideally made with a soup stock made from pheasant meat, although regional variations called for an anchovy stock. To this is added thin ovals of white rice cake about 5cm long. The rice cake is made from steamed rice flour, pounded into sheets, which are then rolled into round rice sticks before being sliced. Finally, garnishes of scallion and egg are added to the soup before serving. Other recipes call for adding *mandu* dumplings to the soup. In the past fifty years, however, obtaining pheasant meat has become more difficult and as a result this is commonly substituted with either beef or chicken stock. This alteration has given rise to the popular idiom of 'having chicken rather than pheasant' (*kkwŏng taesin tak*), meaning to 'settle on something less desirable.'

In the past for the common folk the major holiday of the New Year was not the Lunar New Year, but rather the first full moon of the New Year known as *Taeborŭm* (lit. the great full moon). On this day people would eat and share with neighbors *ogok pap* (five grain rice) that combines rice, red beans, black beans, millet and sorghum. This dish, described above in chapter One, was eaten with nine vegetable dishes. At other times in Korean history, *yak pap* (medicinal rice), also mentioned earlier, was eaten and shared with neighbours instead of *ogok pap*. The significance of both these dishes is found in aspects of

Yak pap.

communal sharing and harmony, and supplicating for an upcoming year of abundance and health, all of which were highly important to Koreans of past times. The fact that Koreans still mark the New Year, although perhaps not *Taeborŭm*, with these dishes indicates that such hopes are shared by modern Koreans.

Another interesting custom related to *Taeborŭm* is the so-called ear-clearing wine (*kwibalgi sul*). On the morning of *Taeborŭm* all members of a family – men and women, both young and old – would rise at dawn and have a cup of unheated liquor. Through drinking this cup of liquor it was believed that the upcoming year would be free from ear ailments and that it would allow those who partook of the liquor to hear lucky news throughout the year. Various types of liquor were used for this practice, ranging from rice wines to the distilled *soju*, depending upon time and place.

The third day of the third lunar month (*Samjitnal*) is another occasion that is marked by a special food. This time of year is generally when the swallows return from the south and thus marks the advent of spring and the beginning of the farming season in earnest. The most representative food prepared on this day is *hwajŏn*, a flower cake. The dough of glutinous rice is pounded into small, flat circles upon which azalea flowers are impressed; the cakes are then fried in sesame oil. Some regions then top the fried cakes with honey to make an even sweeter snack. Wine flavoured with azalea flowers is also made on this day.

Another specialty of this day is *ssuk ttŏk*, a type of rice cake made with a mixture of glutinous rice and young mugwort leaves. This has long been a part of this holiday as the Chinese *Songshu* ('History of the Song Dynasty') notes that this was practiced in the Koryŏ dynasty.[9] An early seventeenth-century writer noted that this type of rice cake is different from any found in China.[10] Samjitnal is also a time when various portends for the year are presaged: the first person to see a colourful butterfly is predicted to have a lucky year, while the first person to see a white butterfly is the one who will experience a death in his or her family in the coming year. While the origin of these two beliefs is not ascertainable at present, perhaps the misfortune associated with seeing a white butterfly is related to the small white hair ribbons that women wear while in mourning. Also, folk beliefs hold that if one is to drink spring water on this day he or she will enjoy a healthy year.

While there are other holidays after Samjitnal, such as the Buddha's birthday (eighth day of the fourth lunar month) or Tano (fifth day of the fifth lunar month), that are marked by festivities and special foods, in pre-modern Korea this was the height of the farming season and tasks such as transplanting rice seedlings and weeding paddies occupied most available time and labour. Thus it might be argued that the most representative seasonal food of this peak farming season is that of the 'field' meal (*tŭl pap*) that was served to the men working in the fields. These meals did not really contain any special foods, but consisted of large helpings of rice or other grains, *kimch'i*, side-dishes, dried fish and a thick stew of some sort; also, without fail, the meals would be accompanied by a milky rice wine known as *makkŏlli*. Womenfolk would carry as many as four such meals each day to the fields to provide the farmers the sustenance and energy necessary to continue their labour.

Korea's hottest time of the year is in the late summer and these days are known as *pok* days, a word derived from a combination of the Sino-Korean characters for person and dog. It is quite accurate, then, to translate these days as the dog days for people. There are actually three such *pok* days: an early, middle and end *pok* that are determined by the seasonal calendar and cover a period of some twenty days. Middle

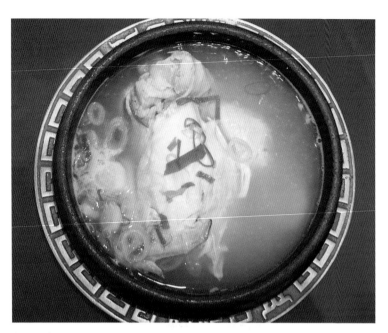

Samgye-t'ang.

pok is ten days after early *pok*, and end *pok* is ten days after the middle day. These very hot and humid days are fortunately a time of brief respite for farmers as crops are maturing and tasks such as weeding are less critical to stronger plants.

In order to combat the heat and prepare one's body for this taxing period, special foods and drink have long been a part of this season. At the basis for many of the foods taken in this season is the idea that the vital energy of one's body – known as *ki* in Korean – must be put into a proper balance with the temperature of the outside environment. Particularly, one's *ki* is thought to be cold in the summer and thus one need eat hot and spicy foods to achieve a balance. This practice is known as relieving heat through heat (*iyŏl ch'iyŏl*). The regulation of one's *ki* has long been important in Korean traditional medicine and still remains so for many Koreans of the present day.

Based on this understanding of the body's dietary requirements, certain hot and spicy foods are seasonal specialties for this hot period. Two prominent soups among many are chicken ginseng soup (*samgye-t'ang*) and spicy dog meat soup (*kaejang-guk*). *Samgye-t'ang*, also known as *kyesam-t'ang*, belongs to a class of food known as revitalizing foods (*poyang ŭmsik*) and is thought to be an excellent tonic for the body and builder of strength. The basic recipe calls for boiling a whole young chicken stuffed with glutinous rice, ginseng and jujubes. Served as such, the meat is then dipped into salt or a salt-pepper mix to taste.

Soups made with dog meat are also popular in the hot summer months. Records of rearing dogs for meat dates back to ancient Korean history and such a practice continues to the present day. Of course, dogs raised for meat are very distinct from the popular pets that one can see throughout Korea at present. *Kaejang-guk* can be prepared in a variety of ways, but is most commonly a very spicy dish. An early nineteenth century record in *Tongguk sesigi* ('Seasonal Customs of the Eastern Country [i.e., Korea]') informs us that *kaejang-guk* is made by thoroughly boiling dog meat with green onions and then adding chilli pepper powder; variations in this record also indicate that some add chicken meat or bamboo shoots to the soup. The work explains that eating such food will not only allow one to sweat vigorously and defeat the heat, but also replenish whatever is weak in one's constitution.[11] *Kaejang-guk* remains a very popular summer dish in contemporary Korea among many people.

Kaejang-guk.

One of the major holidays of the traditional calendar was the Harvest Moon Festival observed on the fifteenth day of the eighth lunar month. This holiday has been known by various appellations through the centuries, such as *Kawi*, but nowadays is most commonly referred to as *Ch'usŏk*. This marks the end of the summer farming season and is a period of abundance and celebration. People were able to pass time enjoying traditional wrestling matches (*ssirŭm*) or simply the cooler weather of early autumn. The most representative foods of this holiday are *songp'yŏn*, a type of rice cake that is filled with red beans and steamed on pine needles, and various rice wines made with the newly harvested rice.

In this time of abundance, food was shared among households and even with those of lower status such as slaves or servants. This was done as a means to build harmony and offer gratitude to those who helped in the farming tasks of the past season. Such goodwill even extended to the oxen that helped plough the fields, at least figuratively, through a game known as 'Ox-play' (*so nori*), which was part of the festivities on both *Ch'usŏk* and *Taeborŭm*. In this game, two youngsters would don a straw mat and visit neighbourhood homes pretending to be a hungry ox. Arriving they would shout, 'The neighbour's ox is hungry and has come for some straw fodder and rice water!' The house would welcome them in and provide the youngsters with a snack or meal. Such a routine

P'at chuk.

would continue from house to house and was a means of both enjoyably passing the holiday and petitioning the supernatural for an abundant harvest. Further, we can note the communal reciprocity that such a game would foster and the importance of working together in farming life.

The eleventh lunar month is the month of the winter solstice, the shortest day of the year. The representative food of this season is red bean porridge (*p'at chuk*); this is made by boiling red beans until they are fully cooked, smashing the beans and then adding balls of glutinous rice to create a porridge. Some variations also add noodles to the porridge. Upper-status families would have first offered bowls of this porridge at their family shrine in a small rite to the family's ancestors and then offered bowls throughout the house to drive off any baneful spirits that might be present. Commoner families would have also offered bowls of the porridge around the house as a means to rid the family of malevolent forces. It was the red colour of the porridge that was believed effective in driving off bad influences. The origins of these beliefs are perhaps first found in the following ancient Chinese tale: 'A [Chinese] man by the name of Gong-gong had an unworthy son who died on the winter solstice and became an evil disease-causing spirit. However, this spirit was afraid of the color red, so the people began to avoid this spirit by smearing red bean porridge on the gate posts of their homes.'[12] Other stories and practices in Korea have long verified the efficacy of the colour red in keeping harmful spirits at bay. Even today, Koreans enjoy *p'at chuk* as a seasonal dish, whether or not the belief in its spirit-repelling nature is still held.

The last month of the lunar calendar was a time of rest and preparation for the busy holiday season of the New Year. While there are not foods specific to this month, tasks of preparing ingredients for the upcoming holidays made this an important time for food. The following lines are from a mid-nineteenth century poem-song 'Nongga wŏlmyŏng-ga' ('Song of the Farmer's Calendar'):

That's enough for clothes, let's now prepare things to eat.
How many measures of rice will we need for *ttŏk*, how many for
    brewing wine?
Grind soybeans and make tofu, make mandu of buckwheat and
    rice flour,
For the New Year's meat, take money from the New Year's account
    and buy dried Pollack at the market.

How many pheasants did we trap on *Napp'yŏng* Day?[13]
Broil the sparrows the kids netted and eat those also.
Prepare sesame sweet cakes and bean sweet cakes, also dried per-
simmons, jujubes, and raw chestnuts.
The sound of wine in the wine jug fermenting is like a stream
coursing over rocks,
From the neighbouring houses the sound of *ttŏk* being pounded
echoes here and there.[14]

Perhaps much like today, preparing foods for a holiday season required much work and expense, but also was a time of enjoyment that special foods made even more pleasurable.

Other seasonal foods have more recent popularity, such as *naengmyŏn*, a cold buckwheat noodle soup) that was once a speciality of northern parts of the peninsula but has now become a food found throughout Korea in the summer months. The noodles can also be made of other flours such as that made from arrowroot (*chik*). This dish adds cold buckwheat noodles to a chilled beef broth soup, which is topped with fine shreds of pear and cucumber, half a hardboiled egg and spicy Korean mustard (*koch'u naengi*) to taste.

In pre-modern Korea ice was reserved for the royal court in the summer, so a chilled food such as *naengmyŏn* was not available to most people and thus this food was not widely available. Moreover, the dish was a speciality of the northern part of the peninsula where buckwheat was commonly grown. However, two events in the latter half of the twentieth century have led to this becoming a very popular summer food. The first is the rather obvious advent of refrigeration that allows iced or cold foods to be available everywhere, regardless of season. The second is the large influx of residents from the northern part of the peninsula to the south in the years after 1945 through the Korean War of 1950–3. Refugees from the north brought with them their regional foods and many restaurants were opened with northern speciality foods such as *naengmyŏn*.

Also popular in summer months are other cold dishes including *k'ongguksu*, a soup made with chilled soybean milk and noodles. The current popularity of cold foods such as *naengmyŏn* and *k'ongguksu* goes against the traditional belief of eating hot and spicy foods in the summer to balance one's body temperature with that of the outside. Relieving heat through heat (*iyŏl ch'iyŏl*) was the measure for summer-

Chik naengmyŏn.

time foods, while the opposite was thought to be true for foods in the winter. Relieving cold through cold (*ihan ch'ihan*) is actually the origin of cold dishes in Korean cuisine, although this practice was never as widespread as eating hot and spicy foods in the summer. Notwithstanding these past customs, in contemporary Korea cold noodle dishes are a major element in summer seasonal dishes.

There are many other seasonal foods depending upon region or time period. Most of these dishes reflect seasonal or local abundance of certain plants or crops and thus relate closely to the seasonal cycles of pre-modern agrarian life. It is also not accidental that customs and events of the year were marked by special foods that were commonly shared with one's neighbors. Such a pattern echoes a dominant trend in pre-modern Korean culture towards reciprocity and harmonious relations with one's community, and also the belief that the copious preparation and sharing of foods would serve to supplicate the supernatural for future abundance. It is interesting that while the underlying aim of such sharing and reciprocity might have changed in contemporary Korea, seasonal holidays are still marked by sharing with one's neighbours, even in the largest urban areas.

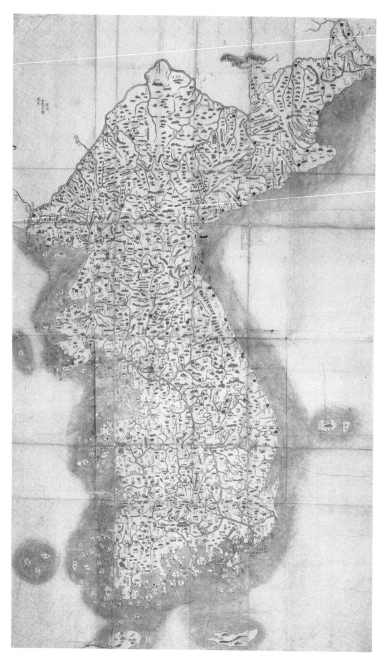

Mid-eighteenth-century map of Chosŏn.

3 Regional Specialities

> In our country Kŏch'ang persimmons, Poŭn jujubes, Miryang chest-
> nuts, Ch'ungju watermelon, Hoeyang pine nuts, and Anbyŏn pears
> are the most famous.
>
> Yi Sugwang (1563–1628)[1]

More than just the renowned fruits described above, regional specialities in grains, vegetables, meats and fish were common in past times. So
too were methods for food preparation and ideals for excellent cuisine.
Even today, in fact, it seems that one cannot go to a particular city or
region of Korea without encountering a local speciality food: broiled
sea bream (*oktom kui*) of Cheju Island, grilled beef short ribs (*kalbi*) of
Suwŏn, mixed rice and mountain vegetables (*sanch'ae pibimbap*) of
Chŏnju, blue crab soup (*kkotke tang*) of Inch'ŏn or spicy beef and vegetable soup (*ttaro kukpap*) of Taegu. The pride in local dishes runs
strong too, so one can quickly run into opposition if trying to make a
judgement on the food of one region *vis-à-vis* another.

Despite the relatively small size of the Korean peninsula, local specialization was common in past times in many aspects of culture including
cuisine. The mountainous terrain and lack of physical mobility for farmers and commoners created quite distinct local cultures. Such diversity is
seen in areas such as entertainment and religious practices along with
food cultures. The survival of some of this past heterogeneity is fortunate
for the present age, despite the ever-shrinking size of the country through
the standardization of culture in the processes of modernization and even
globalization. Local areas have recognized the cultural value of preserving
unique customs and foods, and there has been a surge in the awareness of
such differences among many contemporary Koreans.

In the Chosŏn period (1392–1910), the administration of the country was divided into eight provinces: in the north were the Hamgyŏng, P'yŏngan, and Hwanghae provinces; in the central part of the country were the Kyŏnggi, Ch'ungch'ŏng, and Kangwŏn provinces; and to the south were the Chŏlla and Kyŏngsang provinces. Given the length of the peninsula and the geographical and climatic differences from north to south, cultural differences are not unexpected. Even the types of farming varied, as in the mountainous northern regions dry-field farming prevailed and was concentrated on grains such as millet and buckwheat, whereas in the south paddy-farming allowed for the production of rice as the main crop.

Local specialization was also fostered by the various special regional products that were sent to the capitals of Korean kingdoms. Knowledge of local specialities has been a concern of ruling powers as far back as the Silla kingdom (BCE 57–CE 935). A Silla census register believed to date from 755 provides not only population numbers, but also information on the type of land under cultivation, number of fruit-bearing trees and number of livestock; these registers were compiled every three years, so the rulers were well aware of local wealth and productive capacity.[2]

This knowledge became even more detailed by the Chosŏn period. In the early fifteenth century a countrywide geographic survey was conducted to determine, among other information, the types of local agricultural and marine specializations. The work *P'alto chiri chi* ('Geographical Description of the Eight Provinces, 1432') covers in great detail the specific local products of every administrative district of the entire country.[3] This information was greatly expanded in the sixteenth century as *Sinjŭng Tongguk yŏji sŭngnam* ('Supplemented and Expanded Survey of the Geography of the Eastern Country') which contains lengthy lists of the special products of not only individual provinces, but of each township and country within the province. The listing for today's southern Chŏlla Province, for example, has twenty-seven administrative subdivisions; the individual sections detail which marine products, vegetables, fruits, teas and other goods were found in that particular area.[4] Clearly, local products and specializations are a long-standing tradition in Korea.

The flavour or seasonings of foods in different regions is also closely related to climate. In the northern areas where the summers are short and the winters long, food tends to be less salty and spicy than in the

Various types of *chŏtkal* at an open-air market.

southern regions. Generous portions and numerous side-dishes are strong characteristics of northern meals which help provide the body with sufficient energy to combat the cold. In southern cuisine, one could characterize meals as being spicy and with strong flavours that reflect the heavy use of *chŏtkal* (salt-fermented seafood) and other seasonings.

While all areas of the peninsula can boast a special dish of some sort, this chapter will highlight a few of the most prominent examples. Especially, we will concentrate on those regional specialities that have close bonds with local culture. The order that the regions below are listed follows the descriptive method found in pre-modern geographic surveys that started with the centre, or capital, then moved to the southern provinces and finally to those in the north.

Seoul Region

Seoul served as the capital of the Chosŏn dynasty from its inception and is currently the capital of South Korea. Thus, for a period of over six hundred years, it has been the cultural and economic centre of Korea. While Seoul has no real speciality foods of its own, it has been a centre for the development of highly refined cooking and food

Dried anchovies and shrimp at an open-air market.

Beef ribs grilled with *ttŏk*.

A fish stand at an open-air market in Seoul. While these markets are slowly giving way to large indoor supermarkets, many consumers still frequent markets as prices tend to be lower and variety greater.

preparation methods. In past times as well as present, Seoul is a centre where foods from all around the country are gathered, and this diversity has created a wide array of foods. The height of this culture of excellent cuisine in the past was the foods served at the royal court; these special dishes were then able to spread from the royal palace to the homes of the upper-status elites in the capital, helping expand this food culture further.

In Chosǒn Seoul was further the centre of the merchant class, many of whom were very wealthy. Some in this group were engaged in international trade, and often foreign guests were treated to extravagant meals in the homes of the merchants. Not only did the merchants entertain foreign visitors, but the officials of the uppermost social group, the *yangban*, also hosted foreign envoys from places like China in their homes. The preparation and presentation of lavish meals along with various entertainments was a crucial aspect of these foreign relations.

In general, the food of the Seoul region is neither too spicy nor bland. As fitting its geographic location, the cuisine of Seoul can be said to be in the middle of the different regions of the country. The variation of dishes and preparation of special dishes is what made the cuisine of the capital unique. Thus we can note a greater degree of experimentation with cooking in this region than elsewhere in Korea.

A representative dish of Seoul is *yǒlguja-tang*, a dish prepared by cooking a colourful blend of thinly sliced meats and vegetables in a broth. This dish is cooked in a specially designed brazier known as a *sinsǒro*, which is also an alternative name for this dish. It is originally of the royal court, and prepared in a 'steamboat' pot that allows it to be cooked directly on the table. The origin of this dish is attributed to a hermit-scholar by the name of Chŏng Hŭiryang (fl. fifteenth century) who withdrew from official society and lived the life of a Daoist hermit in the mountains alone. He designed this pot and always carried it with him to cook his food in. For this reason, people called it a *sinsŏro*, which literally means the 'fire of the Daoist hermit'.

The dish served at the royal palace was a medley of thinly sliced meats such as beef, pheasant, pork, abalone and sea urchin, among others, thinly-sliced vegetables including mushrooms, radishes, green onions and parsley, pine and ginkgo nuts cooked in a beef broth in the brazier pot. The ingredients were carefully arranged in the pot to highlight the various colours and then beef broth was added and brought to a boil. As this dish uses a wide range of ingredients and creates an excellent visual presentation, it was considered to be the best dish for entertaining visitors.

Kyŏnggi Province

The central area of the peninsula surrounding Seoul is Kyŏnggi Province. It is also where Kaesŏng, the former capital of the Koryŏ dynasty (918–1392) was located, so it has long been closely connected with the political and economic power of the country. Geographically, this province has both mountainous areas and those suitable for rice cultivation, and borders the Yellow Sea. The Ich'ŏn, Yoju, and Kimp'o areas were all famous for high quality rice, whereas the Yellow Sea

P'yogo mushrooms.

Steamed *mandu* with soy sauce.

yielded a variety of marine life such as shrimp, oysters and fish. Rivers flowing through the area were important for freshwater fish and the mountainous regions were a source of wild herbs and mushrooms. With this backdrop, the food of the region is quite diverse.

In general terms, the meals of past times tended to feature rice mixed with other grains such as barely or millet rather than simply the white rice that was prized in the Seoul region. The mixed rice preference of this area reflects the abundance of both rice and other grains in the region. Noodle dishes were also regularly served with both wheat and buckwheat dishes commonplace. Hogs and cattle were both raised in this area and speciality dishes such grilled pork seasoned with *koch'u-jang* (red pepper paste) were developed here. The city of Suwŏn was a central market for the sale of cattle in the Chosŏn dynasty and with this abundance of beef the city is renowned for excellent fresh beef dishes such as beef short ribs (*kalbi*) cooked over charcoal. Different from other areas that season the beef with soy sauce, Suwŏn *kalbi* is seasoned with salt.

The city of Kaesŏng was a thriving international city in the Koryŏ period and continued as a hub for merchants in Chosŏn. Given this backdrop, it is not surprising that the city is known for various foods. Of particular note and perhaps due to the former international climate of the city is the *p'yŏnsu mandu* (mixed vegetable-beef dumplings) that are served only in the summer season. A Chosŏn dynasty recipe calls for thinly sliced cucumber mixed with beef, *p'yogo* mushrooms, green onions, soy sauce and sesame oil to be wrapped in a wheat flour dumpling. This is then boiled in water, drained and then dipped in a sauce of vinegar, soy sauce and ground pinenuts directly before being eaten. Alternatively, after boiling the dumplings could be added to the broth of a cold soup such as the aforementioned *naengmyŏn* (cold buckwheat noodle soup).

Mandu is thought to have entered Korea around the time of the Mongol invasions of the thirteenth century, a time when Kaesŏng was the political and cultural centre of the peninsula. There is a popular song of this period entitled 'Ssanghwa-jŏm,' meaning the '*mandu* shop' (*ssanghwa* is an old word for *mandu*) that tells of a *mandu* shop run by a foreigner; probably a man of central Asian origins. While the song primarily centres on the sexual trysts of a female narrator, as the opening stanza is set in a *mandu* shop, we can surmise that such shops might have been quite common in Kaesŏng of the Koryŏ dynasty.

Kyŏngsang Province

Located on the south-eastern portion of the peninsula, Kyŏngsang Province is best known for its marine products. The region also has fertile plains where rice is cultivated particularly in the Naktong River basin. In general the food tends to be spicy and salty; also common in the area are grilled fish, seasoned with only a bit of salt. Frequently used seasonings are anchovies and *chŏtkal*, lending to the salty flavour of the region's cuisine. Additionally, when compared to other parts of the peninsula, Kyŏngsang cuisine tends to use more *toenjang* (soybean paste), including a variety known as *makchang* that is used to flavour raw fish, soups and vegetables.

Regional specialities include the food of the Andong region located nearby the city of Taegu. Andong was long a bastion for powerful upper-status families and their conservative traditions. The cuisine of the area reflects this worldview in both the preparation and presentation of foods. One of Korea's earliest extant cookery books was written by Lady Chang (1598–1680), who was from this area. Entitled *Ŭmsik*

P'ajŏn made with seafood.

timibang ('Recipes for Tasty Food'), this work reflects the importance that food had in this area, particularly in terms of entertaining guests. The work contains some 146 recipes, among which are fifty that relate to alcoholic drinks, an important element in treating visitors.

Special dishes of the region include the *p'ajŏn* of the area around Tongnae and a soup made with a variety of freshwater clams known as *chaech'ŏp-kuk*. *P'ajŏn* is a fried pancake generally made of wheat flour into which green onions, oysters, clams and mussels are mixed. The cooked pancake is then dipped in soy sauce directly before eating. *Chaech'ŏp-kuk* is made by boiling freshwater clams found in the Naktong River to create a clear and light soup. Also notable in Kyŏngsang are noodle dishes and various types of raw fish.

Chŏlla Province

The southwestern Chŏlla Province features wide flat plains and a moderate temperature that creates excellent conditions for growing rice. Thus, the area has long been important for rice production. It is also bordered by the Yellow Sea to the west and the South Sea to the south, both of which yield a good harvest of marine products. Finally, the flat

Ch'onggak kimch'i.

plains are at times interrupted by rugged mountains such as the Chiri Mountains in the eastern part of the province, which are excellent sources for herbs and greens. These features have resulted in a rich regional cuisine that boasts many well-known speciality dishes and perhaps the richest cuisine of the peninsula.

In past times the upper-status families of the region were well known for serving lavish and elegant meals. As Kaesŏng can be said to have conservatively preserved the traditional foods of the Koryŏ dynasty, the Chŏlla region has maintained the cuisine of the elites of the Chosŏn dynasty. In fact, the quantity of side-dishes is often surprising to those not from the region. In general terms, the food of this area tends towards being heavily seasoned with various *chŏtkal* and chilli pepper powder and thus is both salty and spicy.

Chŏlla province is renowned for numerous fermented dishes with dozens of varieties of *kimch'i* and *chŏtkal*. In terms of *chŏtkal*, we can note varieties made with anchovies (*myŏlch'i chŏt*), flatfish (*pyŏngŏ chŏt*), octopus (*kkolttugi chŏt*), icefish (*paengŏ chŏt*), winter shrimp (*paekha chŏt*) and hairtail (*kalch'i chŏt*) among many others. These are used simply as side-dishes, to be eaten in small amounts along with

Kkotket'ang.

Chŏnju *pibimbap.*

rice, or for seasoning various foods, perhaps the most notable of which is *kimch'i*. *Kimch'i* is oftentimes referred to as simply '*chi*' in this region. Along with the more common *kimch'i* made with Chinese cabbage and daikon radish, other specialities of the region include those made with leaf mustard (*kat kimch'i*), green onions (*p'a kimch'i*) and daikon leaf and tips (*much'ŏng kimch'i*).

The city of Chŏnju located in North Chŏlla Province is well known for its special *pibimbap*, rice mixed with vegetables. Soybean sprouts are an essential element to this dish along with seasonal vegetables and greens, lotus root, bamboo shoots, squash and mushrooms. These ingredients are mixed with the rice and *koch'ujang* is added to taste. Nowadays this is often served in a stone bowl that is heated directly on the stove, but in past times this was simply served in an unheated bowl. There are many variations of *pibimbap* including that made with herbs and greens collected from mountains (*sanch'ae pibimbap*), but the Chŏnju rendition is famous throughout the peninsula.

Other dishes of the region centre on using skate, a member of the ray family. This fish is eaten various ways, including raw, but perhaps the most peculiar to Chŏlla Province is allowing the fish to ferment and then eat as a side dish or with boiled pork. As the flavour of this is very pungent, to say the least, it is not eaten by many Koreans. However, among locals, it is enjoyed as a special food and often with alcoholic drinks.

In both Chŏlla and Kyŏngsang provinces, spicy seafood dishes are common such as *maeunt'ang* (spicy croaker soup) or *kkotket'ang* (spicy blue crab soup). These and other such dishes mix seafood along with vegetables in a soup base flavoured with *koch'ujang* or chilli pepper powder, and are generally boiled directly on the table.

Cheju Island

Cheju is the southernmost reach of Korea and boasts a warm climate and rich fishing grounds. This volcanic island is known as the land of the 'three abundances': wind, rocks and women. The abundance of the wind and rocks is, perhaps, obvious, since the volcanic island is buffeted by sea winds and has a great deal of basalt rock which was used to build walls and even homes. The rationale for the claim of an abundance of women is not so obvious, however. In past times the women on Cheju worked outside of their homes to a greater extent than in most areas of the Korean mainland. Thus, their being more visible led to the saying that the island had a plenitude of women rather than any actual majority of women.

In past times, the island was largely divided into fishing, mountain and farming villages, each of which had distinct foods. Farming villages centred on raising crops suited to dry field farming, while mountain villages raised crops that would grow in rocky soil and supplemented this with gathering the herbs and mushrooms that thrived in the mountain climate. The fishing villages are best known for the

Dung pigs of Cheju Island.

Hanch'i mulhoe.

women divers known as *haenyŏ*, who gathered shellfish from the ocean. Cheju's mild climate has allowed the cultivation of a small, tangerine-like fruit known as *kyul*. When Cheju was an independent kingdom known as T'amna this fruit was an important product sent as tribute to neighboring states. The first mention of this tribute being sent dates to 476 CE.[5] After Cheju became a part of first Koryŏ and then Chosŏn, this citrus fruit remained an important local product sent as gifts to the royal court.

Rice farming on Cheju is scarce and in its place dry-field crops such as barley, millet, buckwheat, soybeans, red beans, green peas and potatoes are cultivated. Given the rich seas surrounding the island, fresh seafood is enjoyed all year, including varieties not available to the mainland of Korea, such as damselfish and tile fish. Chickens and pigs were raised for meat in past times and an island speciality was the *ttong twaeji*, meaning a dung pig, as mentioned in chapter One. Finally, *kimch'i* is not fermented on the island, due to the warm climate that allows cabbage to be grown all year. In all, the foods of the island are quite different from those of the peninsula.

Special dishes of Cheju include *chŏnbok chuk*, a cold soup made with raw sea bream, and a seafood stew. *Chŏnbok chuk* is a porridge made with rice and bits of abalone. A small amount of sesame oil is then mixed into the hot porridge before eating. *Chari mulhoe* is a summer dish with strips of sliced raw sea bream, chives and a type of parsley (*minari*). This cold soup is seasoned with *toenjang* and vinegar for a refreshing soup. Another popular variation of this dish calls for sliced raw *hanch'i*, a small white squid, served with chives and parsley in a spicy, cold soup. A seafood stew known as *haemul ttukpaegi* is also a popular dish. Various shellfish such as shrimp, clams and crabs are boiled with *toenjang* and vegetables.

Kangwŏn Province

Kangwŏn province is mountainous and borders the East Sea; such geographical features result in the area being a rich fishing ground and also a region where many special products are gathered from the mountains. The area is also notable for dry-field farming of goods such as corn, potatoes and buckwheat. The mountains yield products such as acorns, arrowroot, numerous types of mushrooms and various herbs that have long been foods that provided relief from famine,

Puch'im.

Tot'ori muk.

but nowadays are recognized as being excellent for health. The East Sea along the Kangwŏn coast is where the cold northern current meets the warmer southern current and as a consequence this area yields Alaskan Pollack, cod, squid and brown seaweed. Processed marine products of the area include a specially dried Pollack known as *hwangt'ae* for its yellow colour, dried squid and cuttlefish, fermented Pollack row, dried brown seaweed and dried kelp and *ch'angnan chŏt* (salt-fermented Pollack tripe).

Speciality dishes of this region include a fried pancake made with a mixture of potato flour, green onions, chives and chilli peppers. This mixture is fried and the resultant pancake, known as *kamja puch'im*, is then dipped into a mixture of soy sauce and chilli pepper powder directly before eating. Also utilizing the abundant potatoes of the area is a soup made with potato-flour dumplings (*kamja sujebi*). A jelly made from acorns (*tot'ori muk*) is also prominent. The shelled acorns are soaked in water for several days to remove the bitter tannin and then ground into a fine powder after drying. Water is then added to the powder and heated, eventually forming a thick dark-brown jelly that is then chilled. The firm jelly is then topped with various seasonings; in the winter, a mixture of chopped *kimch'i*, ground sesame seeds and sesame oil is liberally put on the jelly and topped with coarsely ground red pepper powder. The dish is especially popular as a side-dish to be served with wine or spirits.

P'yŏngan Province

This northern region is characterized by a rugged and mountainous terrain in the east, the flat plains flowing into the Yellow Sea to the west, and cold, long winters. Along with rice farming, dry-field farming is common here and crops such as buckwheat, wheat and soybeans are prominent. The major city of the region is P'yŏnyang, presently the capital city of North Korea. Historically, P'yŏngyang served as the capital city of the Koguryŏ kingdom (BCE 37–668 CE) at various times, and was an important secondary capital of the Koryŏ dynasty. If we contrast the cuisine of P'yŏngan with that of Kyŏnggi or Seoul, we can note that the foods tend to feature a simpler flavour and more abundant portions.

Perhaps the most famous foods of this area are *naengmyŏn, mandu,* and *noktu pindaettŏk. Naengmyŏn* is a cold soup of buckwheat noodles and, differently from other areas, this rendition uses a *kimch'i* soup base. *Mandu* dumplings of this area are filled with stuffings such as beef, pork, *kimch'i* and bean sprouts. The dumplings can be steamed, boiled or added to soups. *Noktu pindaettŏk* is a fried pancake made with green pea powder. The cooked patty is then dipped in soy sauce before eating.

Kimch'i of this area tends to have seafood added to supplement flavour and help with the fermentation process. Different recipes call for clams, shrimp or hairtail to be added to *kimch'i*. While there are both Chinese cabbage and radish *kimch'i* dishes in P'yŏngan, one

Noktu with soy sauce.

variation calls for both to be fermented together with a good amount of liquid, creating a mild tasting *kimch'i*. The winter *kimch'i*-making season begins early in this region and entails fermenting a larger amount of vegetables than in the more temperate southern regions.

Special foods of P'yŏngan include a type of sausage called *sundae* and *naep'o chungt'ang*. *Sundae* is made with pork entrails, clotted cattle blood, tofu, glutinous rice and various seasonings. This is put into a casing and tied at both ends before it is boiled. The sausage is then sliced and eaten with a seasoning of salt, chilli pepper and black pepper. *Naep'o chungt'ang* is a well known dish of seasoned pork innards such as the intestines, liver and lungs. After thoroughly cleaning, these are boiled together with cabbage *kimch'i*, green beansprouts and green onions. After boiling, cooked eggs or gingko nuts are placed in the dish. The entrails of a sow are highly prized for making this dish and said to be much tastier than the innards of a male hog.

Hamgyŏng Province

Occupying the northernmost reaches of the Korean peninsula, this mountainous province has long, cold winters. Given its harsh climate

Hamhŭng naengmyŏn.

Pibim hoe naengmyŏn.

and distance from the capital, Hamgyŏng province was often the destination for those sent into political exile in the Chosŏn dynasty. Rice farming is scarcely practiced in this region, but dry-field crops such as soybeans, millet and potatoes are grown in good quantity. In late Chosŏn after the introduction of potatoes, this area became famous for excellent potatoes. Potato starch noodles are a common feature in soups. The eastern coast of Hamgyŏng features excellent fishing grounds for Alaskan Pollack, herring, cod, salmon and sole, among other fish.

Like the other northern provinces, the food of Hamgyŏng province tends to be less spicy than in the southern regions and the quantity of food served is generous. Perhaps the best-known food of this region is *hoe naengmyŏn* – spicy buckwheat noodles with slices of raw fish. In past times this was made with a small flatfish, but nowadays it is mostly made with a type of skate. This popular dish can be served either with a good amount of liquid ('*mul*' or water *naengmyŏn*) or with very little liquid ('*pibim*' or mixed *naengmyŏn*).

The regional diversity mentioned above has enjoyed resurgence in recent years as local communities have rediscovered old traditions and the value of local cuisines. One cannot travel about Korea without encountering the various specialities, and while the taste nuances might be lost on some inexperienced palates, most Koreans will note and enjoy the special flavours of a given area. Variety and local flavour in cuisine stand in sharp contrast to the standardization of many aspects of Korean life in the twentieth and twenty-first centuries.

4 Drinks

Once back I brewed, in pot-bellied crocks,
A strong and heavy wine
With potent gourd-flower yeast, that
You drank. So now what are we to do?
Yalliyalli yallangshyong yallariyalla
   'Ch'ŏngsan pyŏlgok' ('Song of the Green Mountains',
   c. fourteenth century)[1]

No meal is complete without drinks, and no host would think of entertaining a guest without providing drinks along with food. Beverages can range from types of tea, fruit- or flower-flavoured drinks, to liquors made from rice and other ingredients. The importance of liquors and teas is seen throughout Korean history and has long been a source of inspiration for writers. Drinks were also prominent in everyday life and important to social interaction. In short, sharing a cup of wine or tea was a social event, and thus a barometer of customs within society. Yi Sugwang, a seventeenth-century scholar, wrote, 'People of yore said that one could see the governance of a district in its liquor, and the affairs of a family in the taste of its condiments.'[2]

Water

This most basic ingredient for life has undergone quite significant transformation over the course of human history. Rather than drinking out of streams or directly from the ground, modern society now drinks treated and purified water. Korea, too, has experienced such a change, from a period when the water of each house had a different

Chumak (Tavern) by Kim Hongdo (1745–1816) depicts a drinking establishment of the late Chosŏn period.

taste to the present age of fairly standardized and chemically treated water. Yet, looking back at historical accounts we can see a great change in how water was viewed, as the following reveals.

Kim Yusin (595–673) was a general of Silla, eventually defeating its two rival kingdoms of Paekche and Koguryŏ. When he was fifty years of age, he became the military commander of Silla and was engaged in a bitter struggle with Paekche. An episode in the *Samguk sagi* ('History of the Three Kingdoms') tells that due to attacks and rumours of invasions by Paekche, Kim was not able to return to his house for a long period of time. Eventually, his duties carried his troops nearby his home and Kim's family, who had not seen him for over a year, all rushed out to greet him. Yet Kim, steadfast in his duty, did not avert his eyes from his command and passed by his home. After he went some fifty paces, Kim suddenly stopped his horse and ordered a house servant to bring him some water. Kim took a long drink of the water then exclaimed, 'Ah, the taste of our house's water is the same as in past days!' before leading his troops off to the battlefield.[3] We can see in this anecdote that the taste of water was unique to one's home; such a condition remained throughout pre-modern Korea. Families would invariably become attached to the particular taste of water to which they became accustomed. Such an attachment can be seen in the offering to the deity of the well performed on the first full moon of the lunar New Year where the family head would supplicate the deity with food offerings and appeal, 'Please do not change the taste of this water in the upcoming year.'[4]

The actual variances in the taste of water had much to do with location, features of the land and chemical properties of the water. In the southern portions of the peninsula, springs were commonplace and families could collect water from close to their home. The taste would reflect the chemical properties of the water in a particular location, for example, a high iron or calcium content would provide a different taste than an area with another mineral configuration. In the northern and central regions, deeper wells were needed to reach water, which generally meant that communal wells were commonplace. Other factors such as the conditions of the land – for example, whether it had rocky or muddy soil – had an effect on the taste of water in addition to the mineral content.

Water is essential to food preparation and each house would store the necessary water in a large earthenware container in the kitchen. The women in a household were allotted the task of bringing water from the well every morning. This may have led to the practice of women striving to be the first to visit the well in the morning and making a simple offering, often by simply lighting a candle and uttering a short supplication, to the god of the well to petition for good fortune.

Alcohol

In a valley of russet jujubes, are the chestnuts falling?
And in the cut stubble of the rice field, are crabs already crawling?
The wine is ripe and a sieve peddler passes by, how can I not [buy and] drink?[5]

The preparation of alcoholic drinks can be said to have been steeped in complexity compared to that of water. Alcohol is produced as the result of fermentation; micro-organisms that are in the air almost everywhere consume sugars present in foods and the result of this produces alcohol (or, more accurately, ethanol). The origins of alcoholic drink are not clear for any human society, but probably stem from humans discovering that consuming neglected gruels or tree sap produced an intoxicating effect. From such accidental beginnings, human societies directed great energies into refining fermentation techniques and producing various drinks. The initial efforts produced fermented liquors created from grains; distilled alcohol was probably first produced in the Arab world around the tenth century before spreading to other regions.[6]

Makkŏlli.

In Korea, the first records of alcohol are in the foundation myth of the Koguryŏ kingdom, *Tongmyŏng-wang p'yŏn* ('The Lay of King Tongmyŏng'), which tells of three heavenly sisters sharing cups of wine until drunk.[7] Chinese records also confirm that early societies on and around the Korean peninsula enjoyed alcohol: in fact, we can partly characterize these early polities by their penchant for enjoying drink, food and song in countrywide festivals held on auspicious or religious occasions. Thus, almost in step with the development of agrarian techniques and settled societies came alcohol, a situation not unlike elsewhere in human history.

Despite records mentioning that the people of ancient Korean kingdoms enjoyed alcohol, we do not know exactly what type was consumed except that it was fermented in some way. It is not until the Koryŏ dynasty that we can find records that specifically mention what type of alcohol was enjoyed by Koreans, and tell us that rice was the primary ingredient fermented. A Chinese traveller to Koryŏ in the early twelfth century wrote that Koryŏ liquor was of a heavy colour and potent, thus causing one to be easily intoxicated; the record further tells that liquors were fermented with yeast known as *nuruk*.[8] Also, the liquor of the royal court was clear, while that of the common folk was turbid. This account lets us know that the liquor of Koryŏ had already been separated into the divisions of clear strained wine (*ch'ŏngju*) and unstrained turbid wine (*t'akchu*) by this time.

The basic rice wine is the unfiltered variety that is known by various names depending upon period, location and refinement of the brewing process. This classification is known as *t'akchu*, but other names

such as *makkŏlli* and *tongdongju* are commonly used to refer to these rice wines. The colour of these wines ranges from a milky white to a clearer, almost translucent hue when further refined. Simple to make, *makkŏlli* was the drink of the common people. Yeast and water are added to cooked rice and allowed to ferment, and then the mixture is poured through a sieve into a pot. Fermentation continues and creates a naturally carbonated drink that is excellent for quenching one's thirst. For this reason, it was commonly served to farmers working in fields as a means to alleviate the hardships of their labour.

Yet, consumption of *makkŏlli* was hardly limited to farmers and commoners. It is easily the most representative alcoholic drink of Korea and was enjoyed by all classes at various times, as seen in the writings of Yi Kyubo of the Koryŏ period. Yi wrote a number of poems about *makkŏlli* and his penchant for enjoying drink. While Yi was far from the only poet who wrote of alcohol, drink played an important role in his life and was often featured prominently in his writings. He even wrote *Kuk sŏnsaeng-jŏn* ('The Tale of Master Malt'), a pseudo-biography that personified liquor.

Beyond simply a drink to be enjoyed in one's leisure, alcoholic drinks were also an important component of hospitality in pre-modern Korea. Guests were always treated to drinks and this was the measure of a good host or hostess. An exemplary wife of late Chosŏn was Lady Chang of Andong (1598–1680), who is appraised by many scholars as the model of an excellent wife and hostess. In her aforementioned cookbook *Ŭmsik timibang* ('Recipes for Tasty Food'), 54 of the 146 recipes are for alcoholic drinks of various types. Serving alcoholic

Farmers, and a pseudo farmer, enjoying *makkŏlli* with their lunch in south-western Korea.

drinks to guests and visitors was a means by which hospitality was demonstrated. The following *sijo*-style poem, written by one of the great masters of poetry in Chosŏn, Chŏng Ch'ŏl (1536–1593), shows a small part of the social function of drink:

> Over the hill at the house of Sŏng Kwŏllong, yesterday I heard of
>   wine being ripened.
> I kicked a lying cow and put a blanket on it to ride;
> Boy, is your master Kwŏllong home? Tell him Chŏng Chwasu has
>   come.[9]

The maturing of good wine was a time for visits and sharing, and a means to renew and strengthen friendships. The poet in the above poem simply writes of a common event, that is, to share a drink with those nearby.

If *makkŏlli* was the base drink, then *ch'ŏngju* was the noble drink. This clear, refined wine is also known as *yakchu* (medicine liquor) although the story behind this name is not about the curative properties of alcohol, but rather the location where a particularly excellent wine was made. During the reign of King Sŏnjo (1567–1607) there was a person by the name of Sŏ Sŏng who lived in the area of Seoul known as Yakhyŏn. His pen name was Yakbong and derived from the area in which he lived. His mother became well-known in the area for making excellent wine and since they lived in Yakhyŏn, the liquor became known as *yakchu* – that is, the liquor (*chu*) of the area of *yak*. The idea that a little drink is good for one is seen in the common saying of 'One

Ch'ŏngju.

glass [of wine] is medicine' (*han chan yagida*). It is also, perhaps, an excuse to have a drink with a friend.

Ch'ŏngju is made by taking *t'akchu* and mixing this with a spirit made from glutinous rice, straining the impurities out of the mixture and eventually removing the clear spirit from the top of the pot. This clear spirit can then be further flavoured with various other ingredients such as jujubes, garlic, ginseng or other herbs and roots. Each family had their own recipes and produced drinks to their particular tastes. There are dozens of names for these drinks.

Wines made with fruits or nuts (*kwailju*) were also commonplace in pre-modern Korea. However, unlike in some cultures where the fruit is fermented with the wine, in Korea the fruit was added to the wine after fermentation to give it a special taste. The fruit, then, is more of an added flavour to the liquor as the taste is extracted from the fruit by leaving it in the liquor for a period of time. Fruits such as grapes or pears, and nuts including pinenuts and walnuts, were commonly used to flavour clear rice wine. Often, these wines were thought to have curative properties and were taken for one's health.

Similar to the fruit-flavoured wines are the fragrance-added wines (*kahyangju*). There are many types, including those flavoured with peach, chrysanthemum or pine blossoms and with the leaves of lotus or bamboo plants, among many other varieties. By adding such flavouring to strained rice wine, the resulting drink acquires a special and distinctive scent and taste. Records of these fragrance-added liquors date back to the Koryŏ period, when flower-blossom wines are frequently mentioned in literary records. The following verse from 'Hallim pyŏlgok' ('Song of Confucian Scholars'), a poem-song of the Koryŏ period composed by a group of hedonistic scholars during the reign of King Kojong (1213–1259), demonstrates the aristocratic class's affection for such special wines:

> Golden-yellow wine, oak-leaf wine, pine wine and sweet wine,
> Bamboo-leaf wine, pear-blossom wine and *omija* wine,[10]
> A nautilus cup, an amber cup filled to the brim,
> Ah, as for seeing this scene, how about that?
> Liu Ling and Tao Qian, the two ancient recluses,[11]
> Liu Ling and Tao Qian, the two ancient recluses,
> Ah, as for a drunken scene, how about that?[12]

Such a plethora of drinks would have certainly been the pleasure of wealthy elites, but other more commonly flavoured wines were easily made and enjoyed by all classes.

The wines that were most commonly thought to have medicinal or curative properties comprise the class known as *paegyak* (panacea) or *yagyong* (curative) drinks. Most often these were made in a similar fashion to the fruit-flavoured or fragrance-added wines described above, that is, by adding a particular ingredient to strained wine. Common varieties were those made with ginseng, cinnamon, black pepper, garlic, jujubes or honey. Aside from mere flavour added to the wine, all of these ingredients were attributed various medicinal

Soju.

properties. For example, wine made with ginseng is said to be a general tonic for the body and excellent for building strength in men. Then again, some writers posit that the terminology for 'medicinal' liquors stemmed from the periodic bans against alcohol in Chosŏn: by referring to alcoholic drinks as 'medicine', people were able to circumvent prohibitions on alcohol.[13]

The representative distilled liquor in Korea is *soju*. The method for distilling this spirit was introduced to Korea during the Koryŏ dynasty from Yuan China, the Mongol dynasty. One alternative name for this liquor is *noju*, which means 'dew liquor' and alludes to the distilling process in which droplets of the alcohol are collected, much like dewdrops. Given the expense and difficulty of producing this drink, it was initially used primarily for medicinal purposes. *Soju* was made with various grains including rice, glutinous rice and barley, and other variations call for adding pear, ginger and bamboo to the liquor. Contrasted with the rice wines described above, *soju* has a much higher alcohol content at 20 to 24 per cent (and this might have been even higher in past times); rice wines generally have an alcohol content of at most 6 to 8 per cent.

The basic process for distillation remained the same throughout pre-modern Korea. Simply, mature wine and lees were placed in an iron pot and the pot cover was placed upside-down on the pot with another small pot inside below the handle of the lid. The gap between the pot and lid is sealed with dough. After heating the pot, cold water is poured onto the lid causing the alcohol in a gaseous state to condense and collect on the lid before eventually trickling down the handle to the waiting pot. The result of this process is *soju*. A common feature of homes in pre-modern Korea were earthenware or brass *soju kori* – several types of which are illustrated here – for distilling *soju*.

Soju quickly became a popular drink once it was introduced to Koryŏ during the reign of King Ch'ungnyŏl (1274–1308). In fact, a group of loyal devotees to *soju* quickly arose and became known as the '*soju* crowd' (*sojudo*). The locations where Mongol troops were stationed on the Korean peninsula such as the capital of Kaesŏng, Andong, and Cheju Island were the places where the production of *soju* was well-developed and from this early time these places became renowned for high quality *soju*. The consumption of *soju* was criticized periodically in the Chosŏn period such as the following petition to the throne in 1490 calling for a ban of *soju*:

An earthenware *soju*-distilling vessel.

While in the time of King Sejong [r. 1418–50] the occasion for using *soju* among upper status group families was rare, nowadays the expenditures on *soju* for even ordinary banquets are enormous; thus, it would be good to prohibit the liquor.[14]

While a ban was not carried out at that time – at other points in Chosŏn there were periodic prohibitions against alcohol in general – we can see that this drink was enjoyed by the upper-status-group families that could afford the expense. An early seventeenth-century writer describes the history and other dangers associated with *soju*:

Soju is a liquor that arose from the time of the Yuan dynasty. As this was only taken as a medicine, it was not used haphazardly. Due to this, it became a custom that small cups were called *soju* cups. In the present day, however, those of upper status drink great amounts of this to their heart's content; in the summer they drink much *soju* from large cups. Drinking their fill and becoming drunk like this has caused many a person to suddenly die.[15]

Despite such occasional criticism, the popularity of *soju* did not and has not waned. In the twentieth century new processes for making *soju* were introduced for easing the mass production of this popular drink, especially using substitutes for grain, such as molasses. However, today's *soju* is again made with rice in an attempt to capture the flavour of past times. Also notable is that small cups are used for drinking *soju*, as described in the above account.

In the twentieth century, beer was introduced to Korea and has become a popular drink, especially in the hot summer months. Nowadays, one can also find Korean-made wines and distilled spirits such as scotch or whisky. As in past times, sharing drinks with friends, family or colleagues is a way to strengthen bonds and relax.

There is even until the present day much formality and etiquette attached with the consumption of alcohol. One should not pour one's own drink in Korea, but rather be served by others at the table. When receiving a cup of spirits or wine from an elder or in a formal situation, the cup is held with both hands, or by a hand supported by the other hand at the elbow. This custom has rather ambiguous origins, but might have stemmed from the need to keep the wide sleeves of the pre-modern costume from falling into dishes on the table, or might simply be a sign of respect. If one is drinking in the presence of elders, it is considered polite to turn away while drinking; this custom, however, is increasingly hard to find in contemporary Korea. Perhaps to the horror of germaphobes, cups are also emptied and passed to other drinkers as a form of sharing and demonstrating friendship. One who

A fried oyster pancake.

Men baling dried fish in
this late Chosŏn period.

receives an emptied cup from another drinker should then finish both
one's own drink and the additional cup before passing the cup back to
its original owner. This custom of sharing cups seems a very old one,
as a twelfth-century visitor to Koryŏ noted the passing of wine cups.[16]
Cups of any drink are only filled when emptied, so one can slow down
the pace by simply not finishing a cup too quickly. The complexities of
drinking culture in contemporary Korea are easy enough to master and
certainly lend to a more enjoyable experience in interacting with others
and creating friendships.

   If not served with a meal, alcohol is, in general, taken along with a
variety of side-dishes known as *anju*. In fact an adage warns that if one
does not have *anju* with liquor, he will lose his virtuous conduct (*anju
an mŏgŭmyŏn sawi tŏk mot ponta*). What this means is what we all
know: drinking on an empty stomach will cause one to easily become
drunk. Perhaps in concert with such a concern, enjoying *anju* is as much
a concern as enjoying alcohol in Korea, as we can see in the following
anecdote from the fifteenth century:

The scholar Kwŏn P'il liked soy sauce, Min Ŭi liked vinegar, and Yi
Chongwŏn liked spicy mustard [*kyŏja*]. One day they gathered at
Chŏ'ngnyang Temple and were drinking as night fell; about half the
liquor remained, but they were out of side-dishes. The three saw that

Tchukkumi pokkŭm.

the head abbot was fast asleep and secretly stole three dishes: Kwŏn took soy sauce, Min, vinegar, and Yi spicy mustard. The three clapped their hands and laughed loudly, saying, 'How can the words that heaven likes what I like be useless?' and drank to their fill.[17]

Depending upon the specialities of the drinking establishment and the type of drink, menu items can range from flour cakes mixed with seafood and vegetables (*kul pindaedŏk*), spicy dishes such as small web-foot octopus stir fried with vegetables (*tchukkumi pokkŭm*) or simply dried fish. Other spicy soups such as *kamja t'ang*, made with pork, potatoes and other vegetables are also excellent and filling side-dishes for *soju*. At other times, meat dishes such as thinly sliced and roasted pork belly (*samgyŏp sal*) serve as the side-dish, especially for a stronger drink such as *soju*. *Makkŏlli*, on the other hand, goes very well with either the fried cakes such as those mentioned above, warmed tofu topped with *kimch'i* and sesame seeds (*tubu kimch'i*) or the acorn jelly and vegetable dish (*tot'ori muk*) that is commonly served at such drinking places. In all, these tasty side-dishes enhance the enjoyment of drinking with friends.

Kamja t'ang.

Tea

As numerous as alcoholic drinks are in Korea, there are enough teas to match them. In this section 'tea' does not only indicate drinks made from the leaves of the tea plant, but also beverages made from other ingredients such as ginseng, ginger, arrowroot, cinnamon and so on. These drinks were enjoyed for both taste and medicinal properties and remain an important part of Korean cuisine till the present day. The enjoyment of teas can range from the complex ceremony often accompanying the serving of green tea to the simple cup of barley tea commonly served with meals.

Green tea (*nok ch'a*) was introduced to Korea in Silla during the reign of Queen Sŏndŏk (632–646) from Tang China. It was not cultivated in Korea, however, until nearly two centuries later in 828. At that time an envoy to Tang by the name of Taeryŏm returned to Silla with seeds of tea plants; these were planted at the base of the Chiri Mountains and from this time tea was cultivated in Korea.[18] The area south of the Chiri Mountains is still the centre of tea cultivation in Korea.

Tea was initially prized for its medicinal properties and was reserved for special occasions. Such a use is seen in an account telling that tea was

Tofu *kimch'i*.

among the items that King Munmu of Silla used in performing a rite at the gravesite of King Suro in 661.[19] Drinking tea was also prominent among Buddhist monks and was commonly used as a meditational aid. Monks offered tea to the Buddha three times daily and drank tea while meditating to keep their minds alert. Temples also served tea to visitors. Due to such demand for tea, villages arose near to temples that cultivated tea – these villages were known as *tach'on*, or 'tea villages'.[20] The cultivation of tea thus became closely bonded to Buddhist temples and this trend continued in the Koryŏ period.

Others also used tea as a means of obtaining enlightenment such as Yŏngnang, Sullang, Namnang and Ansang, the famed four Daoist hermits of Hansongjŏng Pavilion at Kangnŭng in late Silla. Scholars of the late Silla and subsequent Koryŏ period also discovered tea and it became a luxury item that was widely enjoyed in the upper classes of society. Such interest transferred to the government and tea became an essential part of state rites with a special office, the Tabang (Tea Office), established to deal with all matters concerning tea.[21] Although Buddhism as a whole suffered in the subsequent Chosŏn dynasty, and with it tea culture, tea remained an important element in the royal court and was served to visiting foreign envoys.

The ceremonies related to drinking tea at the royal court and elsewhere developed into the customs known as the tea ceremony (*tado*). Various specialized implements such as a brazier for boiling water, bowls for water and tea, spoons, pots and so on were developed to this end. Further, types and qualities of tea were advanced, as was a grading system for the taste of water. In the Korean tea ceremony etiquette is very important, but the harmony of water and tea is even more crucial to the ritual. The famous monk and tea-master Ŭisun (1786–1866) wrote that, 'In brewing, delicacy, in storing, aridity, in steeping, purity. Delicacy, aridity, and purity are essential to the tea ceremony.'[22] We can contrast this to the Japanese tea ceremony that places more emphasis on aesthetics and ritual, often being conducted in rooms designed only for tea ceremonies.

In terms of medicinal value, green tea has been widely praised in recent years for anti-carcinogenic qualities. It is also said to relieve stress and provide relaxation to the body. Tea should be steeped in boiled water, but not boiled in water. While strength of flavour depends on individual taste, generally two grams of tea is sufficient per 200 millilitres of water. Water temperature should be about 80 degrees Celsius and tea should be steeped in a lidded pot for two to three minutes before serving.

Other common teas in Korea are those made with ginseng, arrow-root, quince, citron, ginger, persimmon leaves, cinnamon, jujubes, Job's tears leaves and *omija*.[23] All of these teas are ascribed certain medicinal qualities: ginseng has long been regarded as a general panacea, arrow-root is said to be effective in alleviating fevers, quince to relieve muscle

Green tea.

spasms, citron for ridding the body of cold symptoms, ginger is good for colds and coughs, persimmon leaves are said to reduce high blood pressure, cinnamon helps strengthen the stomach and improves blood circulation, jujubes are said to posses anti-aging properties, Job's tears leaves are thought to be an anti-carcinogenic and to enhance stamina and *omija* is good for increasing the appetite and facilitating the body's metabolism.[24] While the medical attributes of these teas are the subject of ongoing research, those who enjoy particular teas are quite adamant in their beliefs of the healthy properties of these drinks.

Along with the many teas taken for health are seasonal teas enjoyed at certain times of the year when various plants and fruits are available. This category includes teas made with the fruits such as apricots, plums and persimmons. In general these teas are made with simply the fruit and water, making preparation simple. Another interesting tea is *kukhwach'a*, made with the flowers of the Rose of Sharon, the national flower of South Korea. This hardy plant has long been a symbol of the perseverance of the Korean people. In the colonial period the Japanese colonial government is said to have tried to eradicate this plant in some areas, but such actions only caused more determined efforts by Koreans to cultivate the plant. Tea made from this flower has a delicate fragrance that invokes images of walking through autumn fields surrounded by these beautiful plants.

Given the prominence of rice in Korean cuisine, we should not be surprised that a rice beverage is also a favorite. *Sikhye*, a cold beverage

Kukhwach'a.

Sikhye.

made from fermented rice, is a summer favourite. This drink has a sweet flavour that is enhanced by the flavour of rice, creating a refreshing treat.

A final beverage that bears mention is the ubiquitous barley tea (*pori ch'a*). While becoming less commonplace in contemporary Korea, serving barley tea along with a meal was for long standard. Perhaps due to the poor taste of water in general, barley tea – made by boiling water and roasted barley – often accompanied meals in place of simply water. Nowadays, purified water is the norm for homes and restaurants, but barley tea is still favoured by many Koreans. The flavour of this tea – served either hot or cold – is not strong, but delicately savoury. The Korean term for this is *koso hada*; this term is used to describe foods and drinks, such as barley tea, that have a pleasingly subtle taste that one must really experience to fully understand.

5 Foods of the Royal Palace

With layers of silk curtains and many ply of cloud-motif folding
screens, what could there be to worry about? Liquor plentiful as
a river and meats piled up as a levee, what is the worry to serve?
Unyŏng-jŏn ('The Tale of Unyŏng', early seventeenth century)[1]

Food and drink served at the royal palace were designed to match the
opulence and prestige of the atmosphere surrounding the rulers of the
country. Copious amounts of food and drink were the norm and
matched the other trappings of the palace, as seen in the short excerpt
above, from an early seventeenth-century novel. Historical records
reveal that extravagant banquets were often held at the royal palaces of
past Korean kingdoms. For example, in 674 in the Silla kingdom the
man-made Anapchi Lake was completed with various pavilions and
halls to host huge banquets, complete with a specially constructed
channel of finely sculpted stone fed by a spring. In this channel, known
as *P'osŏk-chŏng*, wine cups were set afloat by drinkers who then com-
peted in composing poems before their cups returned.[2] While not all
of the fare of the royal palace was on this grand scale, it was the standard for foods in pre-modern Korea.

The foods and dietary customs of the royal palace in pre-modern
Korea are collectively known as *kungjung ŭmsik*. The foods found in
the royal court at the end of the Chosŏn dynasty are the result of over
one thousand years of development and adaptation of foods found
elsewhere in both Korea and other countries. As the royal palace was
the centre of the country in past times, it acted as a showroom for all
the best customs of the country. In regards to food, all the regional delicacies and specialities would be sent to the court, where they would be

This is another panel from *Sŏnmyojo chejae kyŏngsuyŏn-to* ('Banquet for the Aged Mothers of Ministers at King Sŏnjo's Court, 1605') showing a banquet at the royal court.

The main hall of Tŏksu Palace, used mostly in the last years of the Chosŏn dynasty.

presented to the royal family. Thus, court food, while not something that the ordinary person would have experienced directly, is still very much the essence of Korean cuisine.

While we know that special foods were served and lavish feasts held at the royal palaces of kingdoms such as Silla, Paekche and Koguryŏ, the present-day researcher is confronted with a dearth of records concerning the actual foods served. For example, a record in the *Samguk yusa* ('Memorabilia of the Three Kingdoms') tells of a feast held by King Munmu (r. 661–81) in which there were fifty types of food served, yet there is no specific mention of the actual foods enjoyed.[3] Records are more concrete for Koryŏ, but the chronological proximity of Chosŏn has resulted in the greatest number of records and thus this period provides us with the best picture of cuisine at the royal palace.

The influence of royal court customs did extend beyond the palace to non-royals. One such instance is the treatment of wedding foods and serving customs among the upper-status group in Chosŏn. As Chosŏn had legal measures prohibiting marriage among those with the same surname and clan seat, members of the royal family necessarily married outside of the royal family and with members of the *yangban* status group. Consequently, in the process of marriage ceremonies, the customs of the palace were opened to the *yangban* families who subsequently adopted these in their own marriage ceremonies. Civil officials, also of *yangban* status, further attended royal banquets and took these food customs outside of the palace. Accordingly, what might have once been the exclusive preserve of the palace soon filtered out to the upper reaches of Chosŏn society. From the *yangban* status group this food culture was transferred to other status groups; thus, when examining any of the major life rituals such as marriage or ancestor rites, or seasonal foods, we can find the influence of palace food customs.

The attention given to food and food preparation at the royal palaces of Chosŏn and Koryŏ bespeaks the significance that food held. Within the Six Ministries (Yukcho) of the Chosŏn dynasty – these Ministries were the administrative units of the central government and thus the highest civilian institutions in Chosŏn – there were numerous official positions that were charged with matters related to the foods and drinks of the royal court. For example, attached to the Board of Personnel (*Ijo*) were positions charged with the procurement of rice and the preparation of meals for the royal family; the Board of Rites (*Yejo*) had positions

Chŏnbok-hoe, raw, sliced abalone.

responsible for the preparation of foods for ancestor rites, for providing wines and other beverages to the court, and with medicinal foods.[4] Moreover, beyond the official posts charged with overseeing the procurement, preparation and serving of food, there were hundreds of palace women and slaves performing the actual tasks of preparing and serving food to the royals. There were positions for very specific tasks such as the preparation of tofu, liquor, tea and *ttŏk* (rice cakes). This complex system was even formalized in the legal codes of Chosŏn. Given this amount of attention, it is no wonder that the foods of the royal palace are considered by many to be at the zenith of Korean cuisine.

Injŏlmi, rice cakes made with glutinous rice.

The master cooks of the Chosŏn dynasty were the palace women. These women had origins in either commoner or low-born families and entered service at the royal palace generally around the age of twelve or thirteen, but on occasion some were as young as four. They were actual government employees of Chosŏn, and are a relatively rare example of female government workers in pre-modern Korea. However, they were not employees in the modern sense as they could not opt out of their positions; instead they were employed at the palace for life. At any given time, there were about 600 palace women of different official grades filling various capacities at the royal palaces of Chosŏn. Among these women there were a few positions that were exclusively dedicated to the preparation of food located with either the *Saenggwa-bang* ('Bureau of special foods') or *Soju-bang* ('Bureau of cooking foods').[5]

The young women who were charged with the preparation of food at the palace served an apprenticeship under senior women from the time they entered the palace until the time of their coming-of-age ceremony. This apprenticeship could last from seven to ten or more years. At their coming-of-age ceremony they would then be conferred an official rank and position, thus beginning their life at the palace as a cook. Palace women were not allowed to marry unless granted the right to do so by the king. Most spent their entire lives at the palace as unmarried women.

At times of large banquets, the palace women cooks were assisted by outside male cooks. These men lived outside the palace and were only allowed to enter the palace on the occasion of a large banquet. The status of these men was quite different from that of the palace women and they married and raised families outside of the palace. In general, their sons followed the career of their fathers and created a class of hereditary cooks who prepared the special foods of the royal palace.

In general, meals served to the royal family can be characterized by great variety of dishes and cooking methods. Whereas commoners or even upper-status families would eat meals of fairly regular and seasonal ingredients, those of the royal palace offered significant variation from meal to meal. Such a situation, naturally, reflects the economic capacity of the royal palace and its ability to cull products from the entire country. Each of the governors of the eight provinces had to arrange for specific goods from their region to be sent to the palace each month of the year.[6] Consequently, the cooks of the palace had a wide array of seasonal and regional foods to work with on a regular basis.

Haep'ari naengch'ae, seasoned raw jellyfish with vegetables, served cold.

Daily Meals

In general, there were five meals served daily to the royals in the Chosŏn period. Such a meal pattern seems to be one that had been long observed, as a seventeenth-century entry in the dynastic records states that this was a practice from antiquity.[7] Of these, three meals would be full meals while the meals served in the afternoon and after dinner would be light.

The first meal of the day was the *miŭm sang*, served at sunrise. This meal was only served on those days when the king and queen were not taking herbal medicines. This relatively light meal consisted of a number of rice porridges (*chuk*) which would vary depending on season. Porridges served include those made with abalone, white rice, mushrooms, pine nuts and sesame, among many others. Side-dishes such as chopped-radish *kimch'i*, *nabak kimch'i*, oysters, soy sauce and so on were also served. While porridge is often a food given to old people or those with illness, it is also a very important food for maintaining body strength and for this reason it was given to the royals as the early morning meal.

Chŏnbok chuk.

Nabak kimch'i.

The main meals of the day were known as *sura*, with the breakfast meal served at ten in the morning and the evening meal between six and seven at night. *Sura* is a special word for 'meal' and was only used for the royals. The *sura sang* (*sura* table) generally consisted of two types of rice, two types of soup, two types of stew (*tchigae*), one dish of *tchim* (a meat stew), one dish of *chŏn'gol* (a casserole of meat and vegetables), three types of *kimch'i*, three types of *jang* and twelve side-dishes that would vary according to season. In actuality, this was not served on a single table but three. This was quite an extravagant outlay of food when compared with the much simpler meals that most people ate in this period.

The king and queen would take these meals in the same room, known as the *sura-gan*, with the king seated to the east and the queen seated to the west. However, they did not share a table as each was served the *sura* individually on three separate tables and each attended by three palace women. The palace women who attended the royals during meals were known as *sura sanggung* and performed functions such as removing the covers from bowls, offering dishes in turn to the royals, ensuring the food was not poisoned or spoiled and removing dishes from the table when they were emptied. The following diagram explains a typical meal for the royals.

Sura sang layout
Large table

A *Sura sanggung* (palace woman in charge of serving the king's meal)

1 *Songsongi* (cubed-radish *kimch'i*)
2 *Chŏtgukchi* (watery cabbage *kimch'i* seasoned with pickled fish)
3 *Tongch'imi* (watery radish *kimch'i*)
4 *Tchim* (steamed dish)
5 *Chŏtkal* (fermented fish innards or flesh)
6 *Chaban* (cooked, salted dried fish)
7 *Chorigae* (a boiled food, such as meat in soy sauce)
8 *P'yŏnyuk* (boiled meat, thinly sliced)
9 *T'ongjang choch'i* (thick soybean-paste stew)
10 *Chaggwa* (fermented vegetables in *jang*)
11 *Saengch'ae* (raw seasoned vegetables)
12 *Sukch'ae* (cooked seasoned vegetables)
13 *Suran* (poached egg dish)
14 *Chŏnyuŏ* (pan-fried fish)
15 *Kim kui* (roasted laver)
16 *Tŏun kui* (roasted meat)
17 *Hoe* (raw meat or fish)
18 *Malgŭn choch'i* (thick stew)
19 *T'ogu* (a raised bowl used for sorting out fish bones or tough meat)
20 *Jang* (soy sauce)
21 *Ch'o kangjang* (vinegar-flavoured soy sauce)
22 *Ch'o koch'ujang* (vinegar-flavoured chilli-pepper paste)
23 *Hŭin sura* (boiled white rice)
24 *Kwakt'ang* (seaweed soup)

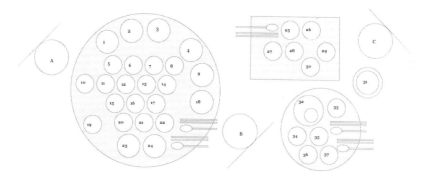

The layout of a typical *sura sang*.

B *Kimi sanggung* (palace woman in charge of tasting the king's meal to prevent poisoning)

Small table

25 *Ch'aesu* (vegetables)
26 *Kogi* (meat dish)
27 *Changguk* (soybean-paste soup)
28 *Talgyal* (egg)
29 *Ch'am kirŭm* (sesame-seed oil)
30 *Jang*

C *Sura sanggung chŏn'gol tamdang* (palace woman in charge of the casserole dish)

31 *Chŏn'gol t'ŭl* (casserole stand)
    Brazier (underneath the casserole stand)

Small round table

32 *Chaengban* (a tray with water for tea)
33 *Ch'agwan* (teakettle)
34 *Kong ki* (an empty bowl)
35 *Kong chopsi* (an empty dish)
36 *P'at sura* (cooked rice boiled with red-bean water)
37 *Komt'ang* (soup made by boiling cattle bones)

As can be seen from this diagram, meals for the royals were not simple matters and involved a great deal of preparation and formality. Even the actual taking of a meal was a rather complicated affair. Before the food was actually served to the king, it was inspected for safety by a palace woman whose job was to ensure the king did not suffer food poisoning, or worse. The king's meal required five spoons and five pairs of chopsticks: the king himself would use two sets and the palace women serving him would use the other three. The spoons and chopsticks were commonly made of silver, which was said to change colour if it contacted poisoned food. In the winter food was served in silver dishes and in the summer wooden dishes. The tables on which the food was served were made of finely finished lacquered wood.

Lunch, or the meal served between the relatively late breakfast and dinner, was known as *natkŏt*, and was a light snack consisting of porridge, a tea such as that made with Job's tears gruel, or a like liquid food on a simple table. The last meal of the day, known as *yach'am*, was also a simple and light offering. Components of this meal could include a noodle dish, milk-porridge, or tea. Compared to the heavy *sura* meals, these meals were much closer to between-meal-snacks.

Beverages enjoyed by the royals range from alcoholic drinks to teas and gruels. Alcohol, despite periodic bans, was common at the palace, and was generally a clear, strained rice wine. However, the consumption

Mandu chŏn'gol, a casserole of meat, vegetables and *mandu* dumplings.

of alcohol by a monarch was sometimes used as a means of criticizing a ruler as being morally unfit to rule. Examples of this abound in the criticism of the kings of late Koryŏ in Chosŏn period documents. In the Koryŏ dynasty drinking green tea was commonplace, but with the suppression of Buddhism in the subsequent Chosŏn dynasty this became increasingly less frequent. In the place of green tea, ginseng and other herbal teas were enjoyed by the royals. Milk was served on occasion as a curative, but was not a common drink.

Banquets at the Royal Palace

Even more steeped in ritual and decorum were those meals served on special occasions at the palace. Banquets were held for major seasonal events like the lunar New Year, *Tano* (the fifth day of the fifth lunar month) and *Ch'usŏk* (the fifteenth day of the eighth lunar month), auspicious events such as the birthday of a member of the royal family, and so on. As a general rule events such as birthdays, coming-of-age celebrations for members of the royal family, or a banquet celebrating a king or queen recovering from illness were marked by smaller-scale feast. Conversely, countrywide celebrations such as the sixtieth or seventieth birthday of the king or queen were commemorated with large feasts.

Yuk hoe, raw, seasoned beef.

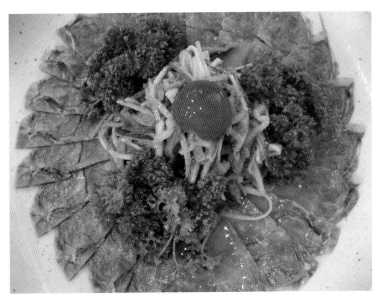

P'yŏnyuk, boiled, thinly sliced meat.

The performance of a court banquet was by no means a simple matter and was governed by myriad regulations. Rules for seating and table arrangements were outlined in diagrams and there were rehearsals carried out for the dishes to be served at the banquet. Other matters such as the decorations, seat cushions for guests, music and placement of incense were all arranged according to regulations. In the case of a large celebration – such as that marking the king's sixtieth birthday – officials would be appointed to oversee all the preparations. Banquets as such were not simple affairs but complex extensions of the strict regulations that governed daily life at the royal palace.

The tables used at the royal banquets were higher than those for everyday meals, and looked much like Western tables. The tables were covered with brightly coloured silk tablecloths and heaped with carefully and elaborately arranged foods. Seating and other matters were all governed by relation to the king or official position: members of the royal family first, then in-laws, then officials by their rank.

The food served at these special occasions was copious, but this excess did not go to waste. The leftover food from a royal banquet was wrapped and delivered to relatives of the royal family and to high government officials outside of the palace. This was a means of sharing the

T'angp'yŏngch'ae.

good fortune of the event with others. Such as custom contributed to the spread of palace food culture as those receiving foods from the palace would then be able to prepare similar dishes at their own celebrations.

Among the many foods of the royal palace, one, *ch'ŏngp'o*, is linked fairly closely to the political situation of the eighteenth century during the reign of King Yŏngjo (1724–1776). The time before the lengthy reign of Yŏngjo was marked by acute political factionalism that damaged the effectiveness of the government and resulted in repeated political purges. As a result, Yŏngjo adopted a policy of impartiality in political appointments; this entailed an equal number of selections for government posts of men from each of the four political factions, known as the 'four colours' (*sasaek*) of the day. This was known as the *T'angp'yŏng-ch'aek*, or the 'policy of impartiality', and permitted the eighteenth century to be largely a time of stability and a cultural renaissance.

Ch'ŏngp'o, a whitish-coloured green-pea jelly, is thinly sliced and mixed with vegetables such as green bean sprouts, *minari* (wild parsley), dried laver, red chilli peppers and also strips of egg and thin slices of stir-fried beef, thus creating a colourful dish. Served at the royal palace, the dish became known as *t'angp'yŏngch'ae*, literally meaning the 'vegetable salad of impartiality' as it also reflects various colours, tastes, and textures. While not as politically significant as the enlightened reign of King Yŏngjo that sought to blend political factions, the dish stands as an example of the blending of tastes and colours in Korean cuisine.

6 The Kitchen Space and Utensils

> From examining old records, it is clear that people [of Korea] have used spoons and chopsticks from antiquity, and this is the custom of our country. During the Japanese invasions (1592–8) tens of thousands of Ming Chinese troops came to our country to assist us, and these men, whether eating dried or wet foods, only used chopsticks and did not use spoons. For how long this has been the custom in China is not determinable.
>
> Kapchin man-rŏk ('Scattered Records from the Kapchin Year [1604]')[1]

Koreans have long had their own means of eating, preparing, and cooking food, different from the ways found in countries such as China or Japan. The kitchen space also differs and reflects the particular needs of both Koreans and their foods. Such differences were noted by writers in the past as we can see in the above excerpt from an early seventeenth-century writer.

From the market or field, various ingredients were shaped into the foods described in the above chapters in the kitchen. The kitchen (*puŏk*) was in many ways the heart of the pre-modern home, although perhaps not in the same way as a kitchen in a modern home. The pre-modern kitchen was not a place to take a meal, but rather a centre where foods were cooked and from which heat flowed to the rest of the home. It was a woman's space in many ways, and some of the arrangements concerning this ownership are reflected in the structure of kitchens.

Farmer's house of the central region.

The Kitchen Space

The design of homes in the nineteenth century reveals a great deal about how society evolved in the late Chosŏn dynasty. Confucian notions concerning the necessity for the separation of the sexes – there is a saying that after the age of seven the sexes should not be seated together (*ch'ilse namnyŏ pudongsŏk*) – led to housing divided into male and female quarters. The male quarters in an upper-status family were located towards the main gate, whereas the female quarters were located away from the gate and within the inner parts of the house. Even in the homes of commoner families, such a separation of male and female spaces was observed, although on a much simpler scale.

One consequence of such spatial arrangements was the location of the *anbang*, the women's quarters, *vis-à-vis* the kitchen. The *anbang* commonly shared a wall with the kitchen, and was warmed by the heat that flowed from the kitchen hearth. Homes in pre-modern Korea were heated through an underfloor hypocaust through which hot air flowed in a series of stone channels and heated the rooms above. Records of this system date at least back to the Koguryŏ kingdom (37 BCE–668 CE) when Chinese writers noted this system for heating homes.[2] In most homes, heating was largely done through the operation of the kitchen

Women grinding beans into flour in a kitchen. Note the hearth and the iron *sot.*

hearth, and the exhaust from the kitchen fire would heat the adjoining house. Thus, while the *anbang* might have been the most protected part of the house, it was also the warmest, an important consideration when remembering the harsh winters of Korea.

The pre-modern kitchen had a packed earthen floor somewhat lower than that of the rest of the house and was dominated by the hearth (*puttumak*). The hearth was fashioned from brick or stone and then smoothed with clay. This was relatively low to the ground and supplied heat by a number of fire holes. The holes could be covered with iron plates to regulate the fire. Above each fire hole was the opening where an iron pot (*sot*) would be set into the hearth. Families with greater economic resources would have larger kitchens with multi-pot hearths, whereas other families might have a hearth with a single pot. Three-holed hearths seem to have been most common. Notwithstanding the size of the hearth, families would have different sized iron pots that they could interchange for different cooking tasks.

The well-being of the kitchen, and thus the family, was regulated in the folk beliefs of pre-modern Korea by the kitchen god (*chowang kaksi*). That the kitchen was a woman's space can be further seen in that the deity of the kitchen was female. Keeping this deity satiated was an

Puttumak.

important task that the womenfolk of a household would attend to daily by simply offering a bowl of clear water and placing it on the kitchen hearth while praying a simple prayer. As the deity was believed to govern the fortune of the family, making such an offering was an event that was not neglected nor taken lightly, and it was generally the charge of the eldest woman in a household. The bond between food, in this case the place of preparation, and the fate of the family is seen vividly in the practices surrounding this deity.

Interior space of a kitchen.

Various kitchen containers and utensils.

Storage room for grains and other foods.

In larger kitchens, there were numerous areas for storage of water, eating utensils, grain, firewood and other necessities. Water was stored in large earthenware jars covered with wooden lids. This provided a ready supply for cooking needs. Grain and rice were valuable and were locked up in a wooden chest: access to the chest represented power in the traditional home. (The transfer of the rice chest key from mother-in-law to daughter-in-law was the final step in the daughter-in-law taking complete control of her husband's household. Yet, this would not happen until the last days of her mother-in-law's life.) Other eating and cooking implements were stored on small shelves, or simply stacked on the floor in any available space. Firewood was constantly needed, and this was stacked near the hearth to facilitate fuelling the cooking fires.

In larger homes, grains, vegetables, herbs and other foods were kept in a small storage room with a locking door located nearby the kitchen. Here, earthenware jars filled with grain, drying vegetables and herbs could be safeguarded until needed. In simpler homes, the drying and storage of herbs and vegetables was done by simply hanging these from under the eaves of the roof.

Another important storage area located nearby the kitchen was the *changdoktae*, the terrace where earthenware jars of soy sauce, *toenjang*,

Grains drying under the eaves.

Changdoktae.

koch'ujang and other condiments were kept. The terrace on which the pots were set was constructed of piled stones, raising it a step or so above the ground. These condiments were essential to the taste of a family's foods, so various customs were followed to protect the various condiments. Sometimes, a rope tied with charcoal and red chilli peppers was wrapped around each jar; this was believed to keep impurities and malevolent forces away from the all important *jang*. Another custom was to cut a piece of white paper in the shape of a traditional sock and hang this upside down from the lid of the jar. As both men and women wore socks, such a symbol functioned as a barrier against the 'traces' brought back on one's socks from a place with bad or impure influences, such as a family in mourning or the home of a sick person. Such traces brought back to one's home would have a negative effect on one's family. Hence, the upside-down shape of a sock reminded those returning from outside to be careful of what they might be bringing near this important place.

Also located nearby the kitchen was the *kimch'i-gwang*, an area for storing winter *kimch'i*. This storehouse, in actuality a low straw tent or wooden shed erected over the buried jars of *kimch'i*, provided a place to keep the large quantities of fermented vegetables prepared every fall. The earthenware jars, buried up to the neck in the ground and then

148

lidded, were also covered with a layer of straw on the ground for insulation. On top of this, was a peaked straw roof that kept rain, snow and other elements away from the *kimch'i*.

Cooking Implements

In past times, when moving house, the most urgent task was to remove and then reinstall the *sot*, as this was the most important cooking implement. This is where nearly all cooking was done, be it rice, soup or another dish, hence the need to have this implement ready to be used at all times.

Records of the Silla kingdom in the *Samguk yusa* ('Memorabilia of the Three Kingdoms') demonstrate that the *sot* had been in use from at least that time for cooking rice. A tale concerning the Buddhist monk Chinjŏng states that before he became a monk his home was extremely poor and he had to sell almost everything in his house to support his widowed mother. All that remained was a *sot* with a broken leg; one day a monk came for alms and the mother gave him the *sot*. Chinjŏng was pleased when he heard this, telling her 'In Buddhism, alms giving is a very good thing. Even though we do not even have a *sot*, there is nothing to worry of.' At that time, he made a *sot* of earth and prepared food

Kimch'i storehouse for winter.

Sot and *puttumak.*

for his mother.[3] While this is primarily a Buddhist tale of a filial son and the results of good deeds, we can also see the importance of *sot* dating back to at least this period.

Three sizes of *sot* were used: the largest size was for boiling water, the middle size for cooking rice or other grains, and the smallest size was used for cooking soups. The shape of these pots varies somewhat depending on location. In the northern and central regions the pot has a rounded shape, as does the lid. In southern regions the pot has a wider opening and the sides and bottom are not curved. Also the above account from the Silla kingdom indicates that some *sot* had legs, at least at that time.

An iron *sot*, if properly cared for, would essentially last a lifetime. However, before using a new *sot* for the first time it first had to be properly seasoned. This was done by boiling water and animal fat of some sort in it several times and then rubbing oil on the inner surface of the cauldron. Rice hulls were then burnt in the pot, creating a black, carbonized surface that made the cooking surfaces of the *sot* much harder. After this was done, the *sot* was ready for use.

Aside from the ubiquitous iron *sot*, there were also pots made of brass and stone. The smaller brass pots were used in preparing smaller portions, generally for one or two people, and especially for entertaining a special guest in upper-status homes. Another common use of these pots was for ritual food: they were used at Buddhist temples when offering food to the Buddha. Stone bowls known as *koptol sot* were of a smaller, one-to-two person size and primarily used in preparing porridges or special rice dishes.

As the shape of the Korean kitchen changed, so too did the *sot*. With the use of new metals in the early twentieth century, Koreans began to use *sot* made of aluminum or alumite. These cooking pans cannot hold heat like the traditional iron *sot* and thus cooking techniques had to be adjusted. Other metals were also used in attempts to capture the taste that was found in the *sot* of past times. In the 1980s electric rice cookers became commonplace in Korea and remain so until the present. Finally, many Koreans nowadays use pressure cookers that are good for cooking rice or brown rice mixed with beans, chestnuts or other ingredients. There is, however, a resurgence in attempts to capture the taste of rice cooked in an iron *sot*. Many restaurants now advertise that they use iron *sot* to cook rice in an attempt to differentiate their rice from that of competitors. Also, rice cooked in *koptol sot* is common at many restaurants and usually features a mixture of rice with various other grains and legumes. As each bowl is cooked individually, the bottom of the bowl contains a layer of *nurungji*, that is the thin layer of burnt rice on the bottom of the bowl, which is eaten as is or mixed with water. These preparation techniques recall the flavour of rice in days past and enjoy great popularity these days.

Other important kitchen utensils include earthenware bowls (*ttukpaegi*) in which stews such as *kimch'i tchigae* were prepared and single-handled pans (*chaenggaebi*) for preparing side-dishes. The form of the *ttukpaegi* has changed little since it was first developed in the early farming societies of ancient Korea. These bowls are made in various sizes ranging from half-cup capacity to a bowl large enough to prepare a stew for several individuals. The single-handled pans of pastimes have largely evolved into two-handled pots (*naembi*) of the present day. These, like in the past, are used for stir-frying vegetables, noodles or meat and for a variety of other tasks.

Also important in both pre-modern and modern kitchens was a brazier used for broiling various foods. Braziers were known by numerous names such as *hwaro* or *p'ungno* and also took various forms. Most commonly, these were made of iron and featured air vents on the bottom of the vessel allowing air to feed the fire and facilitate cooking. Other braziers were made from earthenware. The ideal cooking fuel was charcoal, which gave excellent taste to meats. In the present day such braziers – now fuelled by either propane or electricity – are common in homes and restaurants for cooking stews or grilling meats directly at the table. Popular meat dishes such as *samgyŏp sal* (thinly sliced pork belly) or *kalbi* (beef ribs) are usually cooked on a brazier directly on the table. Many restaurants that specialize in meat dishes use specially designed charcoal braziers set up at each table in order to capture the best flavour of the meat.

Although not technically sophisticated, gourd dippers or calabashes were prominent in the pre-modern kitchen in various forms and sizes. Perhaps due to the commonness of these humble utensils, there are a number of adages related to these that reflect fragments of life in the past. 'To scrape a calabash' (*pagaji rŭl kŭngnŭnta*) is a saying used when a wife chides her husband's faults in the midst of difficult living conditions. Others include 'the calabash that leaks inside will also leak outside' (*chip-esŏ saenŭn pagaji pakk-e nagasŏdo senta*) meaning that one's actions outside the house mirror what one does at home, and 'if one floats a calabash upside down in the water jar, the boat will turn upside down' (*multok-e pagaji rŭl ŏp'ŏ ttŭiumyŏn paega ŏp'ŏjinta*) meaning that the wife or family of a fisherman should not put the calabash upside down in the water jar or the same will happen to the boat at sea. The first saying above demonstrates the close relationship between womenfolk and the ubiquitous gourd dippers found throughout the house, and the second is generally used to criticize someone who nags or talks too much by stating that what they do at home reflects how they act outside of the home. The final saying demonstrates the danger inherent in fishing and one practice associated with hoping for the well-being of menfolk out at sea.

There was also the folk custom of buying a bamboo or mesh ladle on the first full moon of the lunar New Year. These ladles, known as *chori*, were used to sift stones and other impurities from rice. However, on this festive day, peddlers would go about selling 'luck' *chori* (*pok chori*). The origins of this custom probably stem from the function of the ladle: if one bought a luck ladle on the first full moon, one would bring luck into the house by using it to sift rice in the forthcoming year.

Kitchens were also stocked with a variety of smaller water jars, small earthenware jars, straw or cloth head rests (*ttoari*), knives of various sizes and large brass or metal basins. All these items were used for the preparation of food. The *ttoari* are pads that women would place on their heads when carrying heavy food trays to the house or field, or when carrying water jars.

Other more specialized kitchen equipment includes pestles and mortars used for pounding grains, millstones for grinding grains, winnows for sifting grain, mallets for pounding steamed rice to make rice cakes and rice cake presses. Crude mortars were used in ancient societies in Korea through the present. A folksong from the Koryŏ dynasty tells of milling grain:

> Let's pound grain with a crash, *hiyae*
> Let's cook unhulled rice, *hiyahae*
> And present it to mother and father, *hiyahae*
> If any remains, I'll eat it, *hiyahae hiyahae!*[4]

Stone mortars and millstones were common and were used to pulverize grains and other foods to make flour. The size of millstones could range from a very large design, requiring an ox to drive it in circles, to smaller models used within the home. Heavy wooden mallets made from hardwood were used to pound rice in order to make rice cakes, while rice cake presses are the forms where the pounded rice is put in order to create auspicious designs and shapes. The presses were mostly

Communal grain mill.

made from wood, although porcelain was also used. A specially designed earthenware steamer used for making *siru ttŏk* (steamed rice cakes) was also a common feature in kitchens.

Eating Utensils

It has been suggested that cultures around the globe can be largely divided into three groups based on how they eat food: there are those cultures that stab food with a utensil like a fork, others pick up their food with chopsticks, and still others simply eat with their hands. While this might be overly simplistic, it does demonstrate that there are different socially acceptable means of bringing one's food from a plate or bowl to the mouth. In Korea, as with much of Northeast Asia, chopsticks are the norm for eating food. For the visitor unacquainted with using chopsticks, eating can seem a challenge of epic proportions. However, a little practice makes this an easy task.

Chopsticks are a good starting point for a discussion of eating utensils. Korean chopsticks are different from those of either China or Japan. Chinese chopsticks tend to be elongated with blunt points and those of Japan shorter and with relatively sharp ends. In Korea, chopsticks are traditionally somewhere between these two models: shorter than those of China and without the pointy ends of the Japanese chopsticks. Korean chopsticks are also flatter than either Chinese or Japanese ones.

Silver spoon and chopsticks.

Moreover, Korean chopsticks are commonly made of a metal such as silver or brass, whereas those of China are frequently made of bamboo and those of Japan of a lacquered wood. This holds true today too, although at times wooden chopsticks are used in eating noodles.

Chopsticks are always accompanied by a spoon at meals. The spoon, longer and with a shallower bowl than a Western spoon, is also made of a metal such as silver or brass. In general, spoons and chopsticks are used in matched pairs and in more formal meals are placed on a small porcelain rest before food is served. These days spoon and chopstick sets are made in various materials, from very expensive silver or gold to relatively inexpensive stainless steel.

An old custom relating to chopsticks concerns the visits of upper-status group males to *kisaeng* houses. *Kisaeng* were female entertainers in pre-modern Korea, not entirely unlike the better chronicled *geisha* of Japan. Primarily skilled entertainers, *kisaeng* were trained in music, song, poetry, dance and serving male guests. Yet, *kisaeng* were not free: most were owned by the government and not free to select their own lifestyles. Thus, sexual relations with men were often an unavoidable outcome of their occupation. In relation to this, men would place money on a plate for the purchase of such favours. *Kisaeng* did not pick up this money with their hands, but rather used chopsticks to put it in their skirts. Such money became known as 'chopstick money' (*chŏtkarak ton*) in pre-modern Korea and reflects the idea that money was morally unclean and should not be handled.

In pre-modern Korea food was generally served on a small table known as a *sang*. The table was carried into the room with the food already on it, rather than the host having the dishes brought out individually. There are dozens of sizes and shapes of these tables, ranging from very small sizes that were appropriate for serving drinks and a side-dish, to much larger sizes that could accommodate a full meal with numerous side-dishes. *Sang* were made from hardwoods like maple or the jujube tree, which could be fashioned into a light but sturdy table with a lustrous finish. As meals were generally taken in groupings determined by age or gender, households would have a variety of *sang* to meet these demands.

Serving dishes for rice, soups and side-dishes have been made from diverse materials in the course of Korean history. Also, depending upon one's economic or social status, different types of serving dishes were used. We can find examples of wooden, earthenware, ceramic and metal serving dishes throughout Korean history. Seasonally, serving dishes made of porcelain were used in the summer months while those made of brass were used in the winter; on special occasions dishes made of silver or inlaid with cloisonné were preferred. In the Chosŏn dynasty brass was held to be the best material for dishes as it retains heat longer, and was mostly used by the upper-status groups. At temples, wooden serving dishes, made from maple, jujube trees or other hardwoods, were commonly used.

The use of serving dishes made from different materials reveals the appearance of hierarchal social relations. For example, in the Three Kingdoms period we can note serving dishes made of earthenware, gold, silver and lacquer ware; also, while not extant, we can further surmise that there must have been dishes made from wood in this period. Clearly, dishes made of gold or silver were for those of the ruling classes while those of the ruled classes would have been simpler items made of earthenware or wood. In the Koryŏ dynasty the serving dishes of the upper-status groups were fashioned from either brass or the distinctive blue-green celadon of Koryŏ known as *chŏ'ngja*. The *ch'ŏngja* porcelain of Koryŏ was also highly prized by the merchants of Song China, who traded silk and other goods for these vessels.

First among the serving dishes are the rice bowl and soup bowl, which would both have been present at almost every meal. Rice bowls were lidded and a man's bowl was known as a *chubal* while a woman's bowl was referred to as a *pari*. They were made in a variety of sizes for different age groups. Soup bowls have flat bottoms and also have different sizes depending on the soup served. There are additionally a wide range of lidded and non-lidded smaller dishes and plates for side-dishes, condiments and other foods.

Dining Etiquette

Every society has rules and norms that govern the taking of meals. Within these customs we find many aspects of larger social mores and how individuals are expected to interact with one another. Certainly Korea is no different than any other society in this regard.

Our window into the Korean past is the Chosŏn dynasty, for the most part, as we have far fewer records from earlier periods, especially in terms of food culture. Consequently, when we examine what was considered to be proper eating decorum, we can note the heavy influence of the Confucian worldview in shaping these customs. There

Various *sang* stored before use.

Brass tableware.

is, then, notable emphasis on hierarchical age and gender relations in food culture, as there was elsewhere in Chosŏn society. Some of these customs have survived to the present day, although the influence of Confucian practices is waning noticeably among the younger generations of Koreans. Despite this slant towards Confucian decorum, we should remember that this was not always the norm in earlier Korean societies that would have had been more heavily influenced by belief systems such as Buddhism and shamanism.

An important guidebook for proper decorum was *Sasojŏl* ('Elementary Etiquette for Scholar Families'), written by Yi Tŏngmu (1741–1793) in 1775. This work contains a few comments on proper dining etiquette, from which the following is taken:

> When you see a fat cow, dog, pig, or chicken, do not immediately speak of slaughtering, cooking and eating it.
>
> It is ungracious to serve the guest only vegetables while the host eats meat.
>
> When you eat at a table with others, do not take the meat dish or the cakes placed at the far end and place them before you just because you like them. When each gets a separate tray (sang), do not go after the food of others after you have finished your own.
>
> When you are having a meal with others, do not speak of smelly or dirty things, such as boils or diarrhea. If someone is still eating, do not go to the bathroom even if you have the urge.
>
> Even when the food is bad, do not compare it to urine, pus or body dirt.
>
> When eating noodle soup, do not allow noodles that you have chewed to fall loudly into the soup. When you have rice in your mouth, even when you bite into sand, do not spit it out on the table.
>
> When eating a meal, neither eat so slowly as to appear to be eating against your will nor so fast as if to be taking someone else's food. Do not throw chopsticks on the table. Spoons should not touch plates, making a clashing sound.[5]

The above demonstrates that table manners were important considerations in the upper reaches of Chosŏn society. However, given the detailed list of rather crude transgressions, one could easily argue that poor manners were commonplace in many homes and that this particular author felt the need to rectify improper table etiquette.

Meals were served to the males of a household first. Tables with food were carried to the men's quarters by the womenfolk of a house. After the men of the house had eaten, women would then take their meals in other parts of the house. In a like manner, elders would eat before, although not necessarily separately from, younger members of the family. Such patterns reflect the Confucian view of the hierarchy governing gender and age relations. These customs were much stronger in upper-status homes than in those of commoners who would not have had the space or economic wherewithal to follow such superfluous practices. It is fortunate that these rigid patterns have become considerably weakened in contemporary Korea and families most often eat together at a single large table, although some do follow the older patterns.

In past times, meals were not a time for talk and conversation was largely discouraged during meals. This custom, too, has passed in the present day, as meal times are spaces where families can share conversation. Decorum does dictate that younger members of the family only begin eating or pick up their chopsticks after their elders do so, and that they do not leave the table until the elders are finished eating. Unlike in China or Japan, when eating rice, Koreans do not pick up their rice bowl. Other matters of table etiquette reflect the custom of sharing side-dishes with others: one should not 'pick' through the side-dishes for tasty morsels while leaving other parts, one should always make certain one's spoon is free of food particles when eating from a shared stew dish, and one should also not reach across the table for dishes, but rather ask that they be passed. If using a toothpick, one should cover one's mouth with a hand while doing so. In short, table etiquette reflects respect for one's fellow diners.

The setup of a table is also important. For an individual place setting, from the diner's left, the basic rule is: rice bowl, soup bowl, spoon and chopsticks. Hot or watery foods are generally placed on the right side of the table while cold or dry foods are placed to the left. The rice bowl is always to the left of the diner while the soup bowl is located to the right. Stews are to the right of the diner, vegetables to the left, *kimch'i* to the back and sauces to the front. While such patterns have become modified somewhat due to increasing use of larger, shared table settings, the basic pattern of where to place rice, soup, spoon and chopsticks are still strictly followed by most Koreans.

7 Food in Contemporary Korea

Kimch'i is the dish that has made Korean food famous – or infamous. Next to rice, it is the most important component in any Korean meal. It spikes the rice and titillates the tongue. It is not known when or how *kimch'i* originated, but like curry in India, it's in Korea to stay.[1]

While some aspects of Korean food have remained constant, there has been tremendous change in the past century or so. Even today, *kimch'i* could be said to be the 'national' dish of Korea, as introduced in the above excerpt from a guidebook. Yet, despite this seemingly timeless nature of Korean cuisine, the last hundred years has been one of great change for all aspects of Korean culture. The fall of the Chosŏn dynasty in 1910 was followed by the colonial period until the end of the Pacific War and then a period, at least in the South, where Western influences were very strong. Along with such outside influences, internally South Korea underwent a period of urbanization accompanied by industrialization. These factors have resulted in a modern Korea that is almost unrecognizable from the Korea of merely one hundred years ago. Cuisine too has transformed a great deal in this time period.

At the close of the Chosŏn dynasty, it is estimated that the portion of the population living in urban areas was only about 3 per cent of the total. This number steadily increased in the colonial period and reached 11.6 per cent by 1940. In the forty years after the end of the Pacific War, the percentage of the urban population has risen dramatically, reaching 65.4 per cent by 1985.[2] Such a rise in urban population has continued till the present and has resulted in one of the most densely urbanized areas in the world.

Customers at a *p'ochang mach'a* cart located next to a subway entrance.

In terms of cuisine, the changed countenance of South Korea has resulted in new foods and new ways of providing foods to a highly concentrated population. No longer do most people live on farms where they provide at least a portion of their own food. Nowadays, foods are obtained in open-air markets or modern supermarkets. Along with the shift away from growing one's own food is the fact that basic ingredients such as soy sauce or *toenjang* are no longer prepared at home. These foods are now commonly purchased from mass producers, with an increasingly small percentage of the population preparing these condiments according to age-old family recipes.

Another notable change is in the increased proliferation of restaurants to feed a population that no longer toils on land nearby the family home. While inns that served foods existed in pre-modern Korea, these bear little resemblance to the ubiquitous restaurants that now line the streets. Eating out, something that was rarely done in past times and even more scarcely by an entire family, has now become a part of the new food culture of twenty-first century South Korea. Meals once chiefly enjoyed within a family are now extended to a larger social group including family, friends and colleagues from work.

This chapter will not be concerned with the many foreign foods that we now find throughout South Korea. Indeed, if a visitor to South Korea wanted only to eat Western foods – for whatever misguided reason – he or she could certainly do so without much difficulty. The streets of Seoul and other major cities are lined with American fast food chains such as McDonalds or Pizza Hut, and full-service restaurants such as TGI Friday's or the like are abundant. There are also restaurants that feature Italian, Japanese, French, German, Indian, Thai, Vietnamese and other 'foreign' foods of good quality. Although these foods have become part of modern South Korean food culture, this volume will not discuss these foods in the context of modern Korean cuisine. Rather, I will examine the modern manifestations of Korean foods and discuss how foods have been modified or 'reinvented' in the contemporary period.

However, it is noteworthy that even the multi-national food chains have at least paid some attention to Korean tastes. This is all the more true with Japanese or Korean fast food restaurants that try to create unique products designed to match the Korean palate. Thus, at Pizza Hut one can buy a pizza topped with *pulgogi* or even *kimch'i*. And at local pizza restaurants one can find even more 'Korean' interpretations of pizza and with a wide array of toppings that would surprise most non-Koreans. Burgers made with *kimch'i* or *pulgogi*-style meat are also commonplace, demonstrating the adaptability of these pervasive foods.

More important than these actual foods is how they are perceived by Korean diners. Most of these fast foods entered Korea in the mid- to late 1980s, around the time of the 1988 Summer Olympics and amid the loosening of trade restrictions. The foods were seen by many as a novelty and gained considerable popularity among the younger generations. Perhaps more than the actual foods was the dining experience in a spacious and modern restaurant. Given this atmosphere, McDonalds and Burger King became fashionable meeting places for young people. Yet the food was largely seen as a snack (*kansik*) and not really a proper meal.

The general perception of fast food chains has somewhat transformed over the past ten or fifteen years as there are many alternatives that provide a better atmosphere for meeting friends. Moreover, the present focus on the relationship between food and health has caused many to criticize the foods served at these fast food restaurants as being unhealthy and linked with obesity and other health concerns. While the older generations might spurn eating such fast foods, there is no denying the popularity of these foods among young Koreans. They will no doubt be a part of Korean food culture for years to come.

Changes in Twentieth-century Food Culture

The introduction of Western foods and cooking techniques entered Korea along with Westerners, beginning in earnest in the 1880s. With the signing of various treaties of commerce with the US, France, Britain and other Western nations in this period, the floodgates to new cultural experiences were opened. Numerous foreigners attended the royal court in capacities as advisors or physicians, and missionaries were also prominent. Thus, along with educational and scientific knowledge, came a discovery of Western foods, at least among the elites of Chosŏn society. Among those who helped propagate Western culture, including foods, in general were men like Yi Hayŏng, an envoy stationed in the US, and Yi Ch'aeyŏn, an interpreter.[3]

Another area where Western foods were introduced to Koreans was at the many schools established by Western missionaries. Whenever school celebrations were held, Western foods were among those served. Yet, despite this introduction of Western foods, we can imagine that most Koreans had no opportunity to experience these foods and thus most likely continued to eat as they always had.

Some of the changes that affected food culture in the late Chosŏn period were closely connected to the general acceptance of trade and the transformation of a largely heretofore closed economy. Along with the expansion of the traditional five-day markets to larger, fixed locations, was the presence of imported goods. Various seasonings were imported from Japan, and from Qing China alcoholic drinks, while exports included ginseng, rice, beans and marine products, among other goods.

The colonial period (1910–45) was certainly a dark period for Korea in general, and particularly injurious to many longstanding cultural practices. The demands of the colonial government in this period resulted in great hardships and change for many Koreans. The pattern for most people in this period was to eat two meals a day in the cold seasons and three in the hot seasons. Meals tended to be monotonous, as economic conditions were not favourable for most Koreans, and being able to eat until full carried more weight than eating items of high quality. It is said that those of the lowest economic level in the colonial period could only enjoy a bowl of rice once or twice a year, instead eating cheaper grains.[4]

In terms of food culture, we can note that the practices of making seasonings at home began to wane in this period, as mass-produced

Kimbap is a food that seems to have developed from the Japanese *sushi*. Nowadays a wide range of ingredients are used in making *kimbap* including very Korean items such as *kimch'i* and Western products such as cheese. This is a favourite food for hiking, school lunches and other outings.

condiments such as soy sauce were readily available. However, given that the sauces produced by Japanese companies were not well-matched with Korean tastes, many continued to prepare condiments at home as they had always done. One area that did experience great transformation was that of making alcohol at home: before the colonial period nearly every home brewed wines, but by the 1930s this practice had almost entirely vanished and alcohol was now mass produced by breweries.[5]

The period directly after liberation in 1945 was a time of social turmoil and difficulty for most Koreans. This time of hardship was followed by the Korean War (1950–53) that exacerbated difficulties and was far removed from a time of freedom that Koreans might have imagined in the colonial period. Along with all else, the diets of people were poor in this time. Following the devastation of the War, there was a prolonged period of drought that caused even further impediment in food supplies. In this time of dire hardships, Koreans received a great deal of foreign aid that included food.

Full-scale industrialization and modernization began in South Korea in the 1960s under the direction of President Park Chung Hee (Pak Chŏnghŭi). A part of Park's plan was to increase the production of rice and to increase overall agricultural productivity through heavy production of fertilizers and farming equipment. Notwithstanding the efforts of the government, this period was hardly one of abundance and many suffered from inadequate diets. Notable in this time was the production of bread – white bread made from refined flour – and milk. Also, food from the US – mostly surplus – was sent to Korea as aid;

much of this was wheat flour and this consequently became more prominent in the Korean diet than in past times. Other foods supplied through this aid included butter, margarine and mayonnaise. Such a situation caused the 'rice first' way of thinking in Korea to undergo change, as the importation of these Western foods caused a great change in the Korean diet.[6]

Despite efforts to increase agricultural production, the supply of foodstuffs suffered in the 1960s. One anthropological study of a rural village in the late 1960s demonstrates the hardships that most farming households endured, stating that the poorest families in a village would have to endure four to six weeks of 'severe malnutrition' in the period after winter stocks had been consumed and before the spring barley was harvested.[7] Food production transformed in this period as the small-scale businesses gave way to large-scale production, and the manufacture of foods such as white sugar, dextrose, ramen (*ramyŏn*) and similar carbohydrates became common. Important seasonings such as soy sauce were now flavored with MSG, and the production of gum and soft drinks was notable in this period. Truly, this was a time of great change in Korean food culture, although not necessarily for good.

In the 1970s food shortages in general were lessened, although rice was somewhat removed from the pinnacle of Korean foods by other staples such as wheat flour and newer foods such as sweet potatoes and potatoes. There were even days when rice was not sold in an effort to enforce an economy of consumption during this period of economic challenge. Yet on the whole, this was a time when shortages were largely eliminated in South Korea. This decade saw the growth of instant or processed foods and a strengthening of the quality of foods over simple quantity. Also important was the large-scale development of apartments in urban areas which changed both the shape of living spaces and larger communities.

The prominence of livestock rearing and dairy production increased in the decade of the 1970s. The government made a concerted effort to modernize rural areas in this period through the establishment of the New Village Movement program (*Saemaŭl undong*). The modernization of agricultural techniques, increased mechanization of farms and the development of new strains of high-yield rice all contributed to the beginning of a period of prosperity for South Korea. The establishment of large, commercial dairies made foods such as milk widespread for the first time in Korean history. The consumption of meats such as beef and pork also increased markedly in this decade: in 1961 the per-capita consumption of meat was only 3.6 kilograms, but by 1979 this number had exceeded 11 kilograms per person.[8] One consequence of the development of cattle rearing was the growth of *pulgogi* restaurants in this period, and this permitted the burgeoning middle class of South Korea to enjoy beef on a regular basis.

Modernization continued in the 1980s and the 1990s. The gradual opening of South Korean markets internationally over this period allowed even greater amounts of beef in the diets of Koreans along with other foods. This changed the basic diet of Koreans greatly in the past several decades. Rice consumption has decreased markedly: according to statistics compiled by the National Statistical Office per capita annual rice consumption has decreased from 128.1 kg in 1985 to 106.5 kg in 1995 to 83.2 kg in 2003. This steady decline reflects the increased prominence of other foods such as instant foods, processed meals and the increasing use of bread and noodles in meals.

Along with the decrease in rice consumption has been an increase in meat intake (beef, pork, and poultry) which has risen from 5.2 to 40 kg per capita between 1970 and 1997;[9] in addition to the above, Koreans also consume a per capita annual average of 49.5 kg of fish as of 1998.[10] The standard Korean meal has quite clearly moved away from rice, vegetable side dishes and a small amount of meat. Meat dishes, once reserved for guests or special occasions, are now daily fare.

The opening of markets was not always viewed as positive, especially by farmer and student groups, but this global trend was difficult to avoid. One outgrowth of the increasing pressure to open the agricultural markets of Korea was the concept of *sin-t'o puri*, meaning the body and the land are not divisible. The idea behind this movement was to raise awareness that what one eats is very important to the body, and that for Koreans, foods that were raised in Korea were best. This campaign was, at least in part, a movement to 'buy Korean' devised by those who wished to protect Korean market interests, but a consequence was an increased realization that many traditional Korean foods were better for health than Western diets heavy in red meats and fats. We can also note the growth of awareness in regional specializations in this period.

In the past two decades, diets in Korea have certainly become more varied on the one hand, but, on the other, more focused on healthy foods. The variety stems from both an increased awareness of regional specialities and restaurants that serve these, and from a larger array of

Tcholmyŏn is a dish that is said to have been created accidentally by a company that made *naengmyŏn* noodles. The noodles were too thick for *naengmyŏn*, but were used for this dish. Whatever the origins, it is now a popular noodle dish.

imported foods from around the globe. Major supermarkets in department stores now offer a great assortment of products ranging from pasta to salsa. Thus, if one so desired one could prepare a diverse medley of foods beyond simply Korean cuisine. This is also true in terms of regional specialties since these same major supermarkets now stock products that once were only available in regional markets.

'Well-being Foods' and Traditional Medicines

A recent and important trend is the emphasis on 'well-being', or taking care of one's health, in Korea. While this trend entails much more than simply diet, 'well-being foods', that is, those foods attributed various qualities for improving or maintaining one's health, have become a very important segment of Korean foods. Methods for food preparation, storage, types of food and even consideration of particular body types are all essential considerations when discussing well-being foods. Much of the discourse on well-being foods stems from the wisdom of pre-modern Korea and ideas of matching food with one's particular body type. The early seventeenth century *Tongŭi pogam* ('Exemplar of Eastern [i.e., Korean] Medicine') states, 'When the physician has found the origin of a disease and determined what part [of the body] the disease is violating, only after first using diet to cure the disease should medicine be utilized.'[11]

One important aspect of well-being foods is the 'rediscovery' – perhaps this is too strong of a word, as many Koreans never strayed from these ideals – of the theories of *yin-yang* and the Five Phases. These two theories are used in conjunction to determine one's particular body type: we all carry a balance of *yin* or *yang* along with some combination of the Five Phases (*ohaeng*). The food we take into our bodies should match the particular properties of our bodies; what is good for one person might not be good for another as different body types require different types of nutrition. Imbalance of these various properties can cause harm to the body, and this is the focus of the regulation of these elements.

Yin and *yang* (in Korean, *ŭm-yang*) are the two forces that govern or compose all things in the universe according to East Asian cosmology. *Yin* is dark, female, cold, earth and negative, whereas *yang* is light, male, hot, heaven and positive. All objects are governed by these two forces, but there are no absolutes as all things are composed of a blending of these forces. The ideal is the proper harmony between *yin* and *yang* in all aspects of nature, life and humans. In relation to food, *yang* foods include vegetables, beans, fruit and oils extracted from vegetables, whereas *yin* foods include eggs and meats. To achieve a balance of the *yin* and *yang*, foods should be eaten from each of the two groups. For example, when Koreans eat a meat dish such as *kalbi* or *samgyŏp sal*, they usually eat the meat by wrapping it in vegetables. Here we can see the harmony of *yin* and *yang* foods.

Coupled with the *yin* and *yang* are the Five Phases. The Phases are dynamic and are closely linked to each other, either by regulating or by 'giving birth' to another Phase. For a simple example, water gives birth to plants (wood), wood when burnt gives birth to fire, and the ashes of the fire give birth to soil (earth). Similarly, water can regulate fire and metal (in the form of an axe or saw) can regulate wood. Perhaps even a better example of the inter-workings of Five Phases can be seen in the

Possam is a popular meat dish that reflects the idea of balancing *yin* and *yang* foods. Boiled, seasoned pork is thinly sliced and then wrapped in vegetable leaves along with *kimch'i* and seasonings such as *saeu chŏt* (tiny, salty shrimp) or *toenjang*. There are many restaurants that specialize in this dish and make home deliveries, making it a convenient meal.

traditional preparation of rice: rice arises from the earth, is cooked in an iron *sot* with water on a fire fuelled by wood. The Five Phases also are associated with various times of day and seasons of the year, adding to the complexity of this system.

These Five Phases should be present in all meals as the Phases have import for various organs of the body as seen in the chart below:

PHASE	YIN	YANG	EMOTION	COLOUR	TASTE
WOOD	Liver	Gall Bladder	Rage	Blue/ green	Sour
FIRE	Heart	Small Intestine	Happiness	Red	Bitter
EARTH	Spleen	Stomach	Contemplation	Yellow	Sweet
METAL	Lungs	Large Intestine	Sorrow	White	Spicy
WATER	Kidneys	Bladder	Fear	Black	Salty

Imbalance in the body can be diagnosed by physicians with training in the whole of East Asian medicines by examining one's body type, time and date of birth and the effect of various foods on the body organs. In order to correct imbalances, the physician might prescribe dietary changes to put the body back into proper harmony.

Along with the above concepts grounded in East Asian cosmology, foods of past times are being reemphasized today for their curative or other beneficial properties. *Toenjang*, green tea and many of the herbs found in Korean dishes are now held up as examples of how traditional foods can prevent diseases such as cancer. *Toenjang*, the soybean paste used in soups and as a seasoning is said to prevent or cure a wide varieties of maladies. For example, daily intake of *toenjang* is recommended as an anti-carcinogen by the Korea Cancer Organization. *Toenjang* is also said to control high blood pressure and help eliminate cholesterol, strengthen liver functions, carry anti-oxidants that slow down the aging process, prevent Alzheimer's disease and prevent heart disease, among other benefits.[12] Green tea, likewise, has a long list of benefits including being an anti-carcinogen and slowing down the aging process. Indeed, even if half of the above benefits are hyperbole, these foods certainly qualify as being excellent for one's health.

Toenjang: a health food for the ages?

While not dismissing any of the above claims, one should question as to why healthy foods have come into prominence in recent years. This seems an extension of the overall economic strength of South Korea and a large middle class that is now concerned with quality of life. The well-being movement in general is aimed at improving the enjoyment of life, and food is a major aspect of this concern. The sacrifices made by previous generations under the authoritarian governments of the 1950s–80s gave birth to a much more affluent society that is no longer solely focused on basic needs. Leisure time and recreational activities are an important part of South Korean culture today, and to fully enjoy such pursuits one needs to protect his or her health. Well-being foods reflect this understanding. Moreover, that these are traditional practices and foods from Korea's own past also reveals a pride in things 'Korean' of the present age, something that was rarely seen in the immediate decades of post-liberation Korea.

Food in Korea Today

Food in contemporary South Korea has many shapes and forms, far too many to cover in a brief survey. Instead, I will examine a few categories of foods that have come to prominence in the contemporary period and reflect some of the overall changes in Korean society and food culture.

A recent category of foods that bears closer inspection is that of fusion foods. The fusion that I write about here is the blending of more-or-less traditional Korean fare with Western or other foods. This can be as simple as the common 'salad' of shredded cabbage topped with a dressing of ketchup and mayonnaise served at many drinking establishments as a side-dish or much more complex dishes.

One fusion-type food of humble origins is *pudae tchigae*, or military-camp stew. Born of the post-Korean War period, this spicy stew is a mixture of meats like hot dogs and spam, *kimch'i*, instant noodles, cheese, *ttŏk* and numerous other ingredients. This dish is said to have been created when hungry Koreans took the leftover foods of the US troops, making a stew with whatever they could get their hands on. Another source for this dish is said to be the harsh conditions in past times at Korean military camps, where soldiers created dishes out of any foods they could find. Whatever the actual source of the dish was, nowadays there are many restaurants that specialize in this dish that is a mixture of Korean foods and processed meats originally found in the West.

We also see fusion in the recreation or adaptation of more-or-less traditional Korean dishes. High-end restaurants now serve very elegant dishes that have been refined from the fare of past years. Sometimes this is billed as 'palace' food, but the dishes themselves would come as a great shock to the past kings and queens of Korea. Still these innovative dishes are popular and place great import on visual elements along with taste.

Pudae tchigae is truly a hodge-podge of ingredients. This example boasts spam, hot dogs, ramen noodles, tofu, *ttŏk*, vegetables and noodles in a spicy broth. This dish is generally cooked directly on the table and accompanied by spirits – *soju* is best.

Along these same lines is the transformation of the single course meal of the past. As mentioned in the chapters above, the ideal for a meal was a table with numerous side-dishes, rice, soup and meats all served at once. Nowadays, it is becoming increasingly common to have large meals served in courses, much like the practice in many Western cultures. Salads – often a blend of Korean and Western elements – are served first. While the meal generally ends with a stew such as *toenjang tchigae* and rice, the serving pattern is quite unlike that of the past. This is, perhaps, a way that restaurant owners seek to find a niche where they can survive in a very competitive market.

Another area where we can find a blending of Korean tastes with foods of another country is in the 'Chinese' food in Korea. Like elsewhere, the Chinese foods served in Korea are a far cry from those found in China. Instead, they match the Korean tastes for certain items. This is particularly true in *chajang-myŏn*, noodles served in a black-bean sauce. While the origins of this dish might be in China, it has become a very 'Korean' food. It is highly popular as both a dine-out food or as a take-away that is delivered by Chinese restaurants. Likewise, other staples of Korean Chinese restaurants such as sweet-and-sour pork (oftentimes made with squid instead of pork) and the spicy seafood and vegetable soup *tchamppong* have a distinctive Korean flavor that would surprise a Chinese visitor. Interestingly, the word *tchamppong* has now become a verb used to indicate when things have become 'mixed' or 'jumbled' together, much like the ingredients of the soup. Here we can see the crossover of a popular food into the language of contemporary Korea.

Some of the most representative foods of contemporary Korea are those that I would categorize as 'street' foods. These are the foods that are served at street carts located in busy parts of the major cities and cater to hungry people who desire a snack or meal while on the go. The carts, known as *p'ojang mach'a*, serve a variety of foods including *ttŏk pokki*, rice cake cooked in a spicy red chilli pepper sauce with strips of fishcake and boiled eggs, *sundae*, a sausage made with beef or pork mixed with tofu and stuffed in a pig intestine, dried squid and snacks such as cakes made with glutinous rice flour and filled with red bean paste. Some carts have benches or other seating, while others are for standing customers only; in the winter months, some vendors encircle their cart and seating with vinyl tarps and heat the interior, creating small oases on otherwise cold nights. These carts also serve drinks such as *soju* or *makkŏlli*, which make good companions for the above foods.

This dish of seasoned, cooked beef and vegetables in rice-paper 'pockets' is one example of the continued development of Korean cuisine.

Tchamppong.

So common are the carts that at night the sidewalks in busy parts of the city are almost completely given over to lines of carts and people enjoying different foods.

The food served in these carts has undergone much change in recent history. In the 1960s fare such as roasted sparrows was commonplace, whereas nowadays one would be hard-pressed to find that particular dish. Some vendors, however, still sell snacks that have long been present such as the pungent *pŏndegi* (steamed silkworm pupa), or the small conical snails that are boiled and then sucked straight from the shell. The scents of the changing seasons are reflected in the food sold too, with cold winter nights being a perfect time to enjoy a steaming hot baked sweet potato, and cool watermelon slices ideal for summer days.

Many of these popular foods have now moved indoors; that is, they are now served in regular restaurants. There are numerous restaurants

Diners enjoying lunch in a restaurant. Note the stone bowls in which the rice is prepared and served.

In the foreground are skewers of *odeng* (fishcake) heated in a broth. Next to it are fryers for preparing various deep-fried foods, followed by a pan of *ttŏk pokki*.

Ttŏk pokki.

that sell dishes like *ttŏk pokki* or *sundae* as specialties. *Ttŏk pokki* shops in particular are nearly always located near schools, as this is a favourite dish of many Korean students of all ages. Also notable is the presence of these same 'street' foods at the rest stops along South Korea's highways. The rest stops, the only places where food can be bought without exiting the toll roads, sell treats like pan-fried whole potatoes, *ttŏk pokki*, dried squid and so on, demonstrating how these humble foods have now become a large part of Korean culture. Indeed, a long trip from Seoul to Pusan or Kwangju just is not the same without a stop for pan-fried potatoes or a half-dried, roasted squid.

Another aspect of modern Korean dining that often seems lost on visitors is the reciprocal nature of paying for food. Unlike the more-or-less standard of paying one's own way, or separate bills found in Western culture, in Korea generally one individual pays for a meal. Such a practice is based in pre-modern concepts of reciprocity where one demonstrates his or her hospitality by treating another to a meal. In the modern practice this is parlayed into a rotating system of paying for meals among friends and colleagues. Moreover, after eating dinner Koreans will often then head to a drinking establishment for a second stop. Here, another person will pay for the tab, and if there is a third stop (or even more) in the evening, yet another will pick up the bill. Sometimes one's turn to pay in a large group might not come up for several months, but the pleasure of eventually treating one's friends allows one to demonstrate his or her hospitality. Treating one's friends or colleagues is also commonly done when a happy event occurs such as a first pay cheque from a new job, marriage or the birth

of a child. These practices stem from the pre-modern practices of sharing with one's neighbours and community as a means to foster harmonic relations.

A final aspect to consider is the new directions that Korean cuisine has taken in the past few decades. The contact of globalization is not always from foreign cultures, but sometimes from ethnic Koreans who have immigrated elsewhere. There are major populations of Koreans in China, Japan, the countries of the former Soviet Union and the United States. These new environments have resulted in changes to Korean cuisine through contact with new foods and ways of cooking. One example of this is found in LA *kalbi*, a new style of the popular beef rib dish that seems to have origins in the large Korean population of Los Angeles. While this is still a marinated beef rib dish, the cut of the meat – in thin segments across several ribs – reflects the type of meat cuts available in the US. This style of *kalbi* is now popular in both Korea and the US. No doubt the future will hold more innovations in Korea cuisine through the experiences of the Korean diaspora.

While it is difficult to imagine the shape of Korean cuisine in twenty years, one can imagine that age-old standards such as *kimch'i*, numerous side-dishes and rice will continue to be prominent. While there is little doubt there will be changes in diet patterns, foods of past times will certainly remain at the pinnacle of Korean cuisine and will continue to be a means for defining an aspect of Korean identity.

Recipes

Main Dishes

Ttŏkkuk: Rice Cake Soup

Most closely associated with the Lunar New Year celebration, *ttŏkkuk* was nearly always enjoyed on this holiday as a means to mark the New Year. This soup, traditionally made with pheasant stock, can also be made with either beef or anchovy stock. The sliced rice cake ovals can be bought in Korean or Asian markets. The following recipe is modified from the early-nineteenth-century *Tongguk sesigi* ('Seasonal Customs of the Eastern Country [i.e., Korea]').

Serves 3–4, depending upon portions

Ingredients
200g white rice cake ovals
1 egg
3 tbsp chopped spring onions
2 tbsp soy sauce
½ tsp thinly sliced chillies
salt to taste
black pepper to taste
¼ cup laver, roasted and then crumbled

Beef stock
300 grams beef (brisket or flank steak works well)
1 large spring onion
5 black peppercorns
5 cloves garlic, cleaned and peeled
2.4 litres water

Beef seasoning
½ clove crushed garlic (for all recipes, I am using medium-sized cloves of garlic: please adjust quantity if necessary)
½ tsp soy sauce
½ tsp ground sesame seeds
½ tsp black pepper
½ tsp salt
½ tsp sesame oil

Rinse the rice cakes in water and set aside (if frozen, allow to soak for 15–20 minutes). Soak the beef in cold water and skim any impurities off the surface. Next, add the stock ingredients and bring to a boil with the beef. Remove any froth that arises in the pot to create a clear stock. When the meat can be easily pierced with a chopstick it is done – set aside and let it cool.

When the beef has cooled sufficiently, shred into small pieces and then mix in the beef seasoning, kneading the mixture thoroughly. Ladle the beef stock into another pan (taking only the clear liquid) and bring to a boil again. While the stock is coming to a boil, separate the white from the egg yolk and thinly fry each, creating yellow and white egg 'pancakes'. Slice these pancakes into thin strips and set aside. Roast the sheets of laver over a burner, being careful not to burn it. Then, crumble the sheets into small pieces (this is easily and neatly done by putting the roasted laver into a small plastic bag and then crumbling).

After the stock boils, add the sliced rice cake and again boil. Add soy sauce, salt and pepper to taste. Ladle the soup and *ttŏk* into individual bowls and top with the shredded beef, egg strips, laver, chopped green onion and strips of chillies.

Kaejang-guk: Dog-meat Soup

This is still a very popular summer dish in Korea, as it allows balancing of one's inner and outer temperatures. This practice, known as relieving heat through heat (*iyŏl ch'iyŏl*) is an important aspect of maintaining health through the hot summer months. One recipe from the seventeenth century, found in *Ŭmsik timibang* ('Recipes for Tasty Food') written by Lady Chang, calls for the flesh to be removed from the bones and thoroughly washed in water. This was then to be set aside. Sesame seeds were added to water in a pot and fried, then pounded before soy sauce was added. To this mixture was added wheat flour and sesame oil, and additional soy sauce gave the dish more saltiness. Finally, the dog meat was added, brought to a rapid boil and then simmered until well cooked. Directly before serving, spring onions, ginger, black pepper and Chinese peppercorns (*chop'i*) were added to the soup.

The above recipe, however, is somewhat different from what a present-day diner will find in Korea. A spicier version of the dish is now in favour, as shown in the recipe below.

Serves 4

Ingredients
800g dog meat
200g boiled taro
300g sesame leaves
80g dropwort (*minari*)
5 large spring onions
Salt to taste
2 tbsp ground perilla seeds
1.9 litres water
1 small piece of fresh ginger (approx. 100 grams), sliced
2 tbsp *toenjang*

Seasoning
1 tbsp soy sauce
2 tbsp chopped spring onions
1 tbsp crushed garlic
1 tbsp Korean fine chilli pepper powder
black pepper to taste

Dipping sauce for the meat
2 tbsp ground perilla seeds
1 tbsp chilli powder
1 tbsp sesame or perilla oil

As dog meat is generally cooked with the skin intact, trim any fur and clean thoroughly. Often, fur is burnt off the skin with a flame. Cut the taro into about 5cm lengths and thinly slice any thick parts. Clean the sesame leaves and cut up roughly and also clean and cut the *minari* and spring onions into about 5cm lengths.

Put the meat and ginger into a large pot and cover with water; bring to a boil and when the liquid begins to boil down reduce the heat to a simmer and cook for about three hours. When the meat is tender, remove the meat from the water and, after it cools off, tear into bite-sized pieces.

Strain the remaining water through a fine sieve or cheesecloth to remove fat and any impurities. To the cooked meat add the boiled taro, green onions and the seasonings and work together well. Finally, add the seasoned meat mixture and remaining vegetables to the strained broth and bring to a boil. Add salt to taste if bland and then serve in bowls. The dog meat can be dipped in the sauce directly before eating if desired, or some enjoy adding the dipping sauce directly to the soup.

Kaejang-guk goes well with *kkaktugi kimch'i* and side dishes such as raw chillies, carrot sticks and cucumber sticks. The raw vegetables are dipped into either *toenjang* or *koch'ujang* directly before eating. *Soju* is an excellent drink to enjoy with *kaejang-guk*.

Kkotke t'ang: Spicy Blue Crab Soup

Kkotke t'ang is a spicy soup that was traditionally enjoyed in the coastal areas along the West and South seas.

Serves 2

For the anchovy stock
1.2 litres water

10 cm² *tasima* (*tasima* is sun-dried kelp used for making seafood stock)
5–6 large dried anchovies (these are anchovies specifically for making stock known as *kuk myŏlch'i* that can be found in Korean or Asian markets)

Ingredients
2 blue crabs, raw and cleaned
3 tbsp *toenjang*
2 cups sliced daikon radish
1 sliced yellow onion (around 1 cup)
1 tbsp Korean fine chilli pepper powder
3 cloves crushed garlic
⅓ tbsp powdered ginger powder
2 to 3 spring onions, cut into roughly 5cm lengths
2 or 3 red and green chilli peppers, sliced

Put the dried anchovies in a pot with the water and bring to a boil; then put in the *tasima* and continue to boil for another 10 minutes.

With a strainer, remove the anchovies and *tasima*; this is your anchovy stock.

Add the *toenjang*, daikon radish and yellow onion. After the water begins to boil add the raw crabs to the pot and boil for around 5 minutes, removing any froth from the pot with a spoon while the crabs are cooking.

Add the remaining ingredients and cook for an additional 5 minutes. Serve as a shared stew along with rice and side-dishes.

Samgye t'ang: Chicken and Ginseng Soup

Samgye t'ang is generally eaten during the hottest part of the summer to give the body strength. It should be served in individual earthenware or stone bowls.

Serves 2

> *Ingredients*
> 2 Cornish hens or poussin of about 500g each
> 100g glutinous rice
> 6–8 peeled cloves of garlic
> 4 jujubes
> 4 chestnuts
> 2 pieces of dried ginseng (about 5cm in length)
> salt and pepper to taste

Soak the glutinous rice in water for about one hour before beginning. Clean the hens thoroughly and stuff each with half the above ingredients (except the salt and pepper). Do not pack the hens too tightly as they will swell during cooking. Skewer or tie the legs to keep the stuffing from falling out during cooking.

Place the stuffed hens in earthenware bowls and add enough water to cover the chickens. Bring to a boil and then cover and simmer for about one hour or until the flesh is nearly falling off the bones. Serve in the earthenware bowls used for cooking; dip the meat into a salt and pepper mixture directly before eating.

A similar recipe for a 'stuffed' hen soup from the seventeenth-century *Ŭmsik timibang* ('Recipes for Tasty Food') calls for adding *toenjang*, ginger and spring onions among other ingredients. It does not include ginseng, so we can see this would be a very different soup from today's *samgye t'ang*.

Chŏnbok chuk: Abalone Porridge

This dish was common in areas by the southern ocean and especially on Cheju Island where women divers gathered the abalone from the sea. Additionally, it was a frequent breakfast dish at the royal court.

Serves 4

> *Ingredients*
> 185g white rice
> 125g abalone
> 1–2 tbsp sesame oil
> 1600ml water
> Soy sauce to taste
> Salt to taste

Soak the rice in the water, completely covering it, for three to four hours until it is swollen. Remove the abalone from the shell and clean thoroughly before cutting into thin strips.

Heat the sesame oil in a deep saucepan and then add the abalone strips and fry lightly. Next add the drained rice and stir-fry along with the abalone until it is well coated in oil. Then add the water and bring to a boil over a medium heat. At this point, reduce the heat and cover the pan, allowing the mixture to simmer for 35–40 minutes, stirring frequently.

When the rice is soft and most of the water absorbed, the porridge is ready for serving. Soy sauce and salt are then added to individual bowls according to taste.

Nŭbiani: Grilled Marinated Beef

This beef dish was originally served at the royal palace. It is easily prepared. Other items can be grilled along with the beef such as sliced raw garlic, sliced chilli peppers or mushrooms.

Serves 2–3

Ingredients
500g beef (thinly sliced rib-eye is best)
4 tbsp soy sauce
4 tbsp beef stock
2 tbsp brown sugar
2 tbsp chopped spring onions
3 cloves crushed garlic
1 tbsp ground sesame seeds
1 tbsp sesame oil
black pepper to taste

Select a lean cut of beef and cut into thin slices of about 0.5 cm thickness. Then tenderize with the back edge of a knife. Mix all the seasonings together in a bowl.

30 minutes before cooking, add the beef to the bowl and knead it with the marinade, working it well into the meat. Cook immediately before eating, preferably on a charcoal grill (outside) or a small tabletop grill. Cut the meat into bite-sized pieces when it is nearly cooked. Do not overcook.

To eat, put a piece of beef in a lettuce leaf and wrap it up with a small amount of cooked rice and a piece of grilled garlic, sliced chilli or mushroom.

Tak kui: Grilled Chicken

This is a great way to grill chicken. The recipe is based on a dish formerly served at the royal palace in the Chosŏn dynasty.

Serves 4

Ingredients
1 800g chicken (or substitute 400 grams of boneless chicken)

Seasoning
2 tbsp soy sauce
1 tsp salt
2 tbsp chopped spring onions
1 clove crushed garlic
1 tsp ground sesame seeds
1 tsp sesame oil
½ tsp crushed fresh ginger (or, substitute ½ tsp of powdered ginger)
black pepper to taste

Wash the chicken thoroughly and then cut into flattened, relatively thick pieces. Mix the seasoning ingredients together and add the chicken, piece by piece, making sure to work the seasoning into the meat by kneading. After allowing the chicken to marinate in the seasoning for approximately 30 minutes, cook until fully done on a grill. If a healthier meal is desired, skinless chicken can also be used in the recipe.

This meal can be accompanied by leaf lettuce or other leafy vegetables and eaten as *ssam*, that is, meat with rice wrapped in a vegetable leaf.

Yak pap: Medicinal Rice

This recipe has been modified from *Kyuhap ch'ongsŏ* ('Encyclopaedia of Women's Daily Life') written by Yi Pinghŏhak (1759–1824). *Yak pap* was a food commonly enjoyed on *Taeborŭm*, the first full moon of the lunar New Year.

Ingredients
750g glutinous rice
500g brown sugar
3 tbsp sesame oil
3 tbsp soy sauce
8 to 10 chestnuts
15 jujubes (Chinese dates)
1 tbsp pine nuts

Rinse and then soak the glutinous rice in water for about 5 hours until it is well swollen. Shell the chestnuts and cut each into four or five pieces, and rinse and remove the stones from the jujubes.

When the rice is ready, drain the excess water (the proper water level is enough to cover the back of one's hand when placed on top of the rice in the pan before cooking) and cook the rice until it is done. Then, before the cooked rice cools, stir in the remaining ingredients and cook for another two to three hours until the mixture is a dark brownish colour.

The Chosŏn period recipes for this dish call for honey rather than brown sugar, but at present brown sugar is widely used. To substitute honey for the sugar, use 320ml of honey instead of the brown sugar.

Pulgogi: Thinly-sliced Marinated Beef

While this is one of the most popular dishes among visitors to Korea, we cannot find records of it in pre-modern cookbooks. Nonetheless, grilled meat dishes were often mixed with vegetables and served at royal palace banquets or at festive occasions in the homes of upper-status group families. Whatever its historic origins, *pulgogi* is relatively easy to make.

In Korean or some Asian markets it is often possible to buy *pulgogi* beef, that is, very thinly cut, almost shaved, beef that is made just for this dish. However, if such a product is not available, very thinly sliced rib-eye, sirloin or tenderloin will be fine. Slicing the fresh meat thinly is made easier by putting the meat into the freezer for 30 minutes or so before cutting.

Serves 3–4

Ingredients
600g thinly-sliced rib-eye, sirloin or tenderloin beef
1 medium onion, thinly sliced
1 carrot, julienned
6 tbsp soy sauce
3 tbsp sugar (white or brown)
3 tbsp pear juice (grate an 'Asian pear' for the juice)
3 tbsp *soju* (if *soju* is not available, a dry wine will work)
3 tbsp chopped spring onions
2 cloves crushed garlic

⅓ tbsp powdered ginger powder
⅓ tbsp black pepper
1 tbsp roasted sesame seeds
1 tbsp sesame oil

Mix all of the above ingredients in a large bowl, making certain to knead the marinade well into the meat. Allow the entire mixture to sit for about 30 minutes before cooking.

While *pulgogi* can be cooked directly over a flame on a grill, this particular recipe is excellent for cooking in a frying pan. Do not drain the juice, and serve in the cooking pan on the tabletop. The *pulgogi* should not be overcooked and can be eaten wrapped in lettuce with rice, or just by itself. When several spoonfuls of the juice is added to individual servings of rice, it makes a very tasty dish.

Other vegetables can be added to this recipe such as enoki mushrooms (*p'aengi pŏsŏt*) or green peppers. The wrapped *pulgogi* in lettuce leaves can be further augmented with *koch'ujang* or *toenjang*.

Kimch'i tchigae: *Kimch'i* Stew

Kimch'i never goes to waste in a Korean home. However, after it becomes sour it does not make such a good side-dish. One way to utilize sour *kimch'i* and create a very tasty stew is by making *kimch'i tchigae*, a staple in most every Korean home. Commonly this is cooked and served in an unglazed earthenware pot known as a *ttukpaegi*, which can be found in Korean markets.

Serves 2–3

Ingredients
1 tbsp cooking oil (canola oil is often used in Korean cooking)
100g pork
400g sour (*paech'u*) *kimch'i*
550 ml water
100g firm tofu, cut into small cubes
1 large spring onion, cut into 5cm lengths
½ clove crushed garlic
½ tbsp Korean fine chilli pepper powder
salt to taste

Do not rinse the *kimch'i*, but cut it into about 3cm lengths and set aside. The pork should be cut into bite-sized pieces and then put into the pot and stir-fried in the oil. Alternatively, a small amount of water can also be used to brown the pork.

Next, add the cut *kimch'i* and stir-fry lightly for a minute or two before adding the water. Some recipes call for adding anchovy stock rather than water – if desired, see the directions for preparing anchovy stock under the recipe for *kkotke t'ang* above. Still other cooks like to add about 1 cup of juice from the *kimch'i* jar in place of 1 cup of the water.

After the *kimch'i* and pork come to a boil, add the remaining ingredients and boil for about 5 minutes. If the soup is bland, add salt, and if it is too sour, add ½ tbsp of brown sugar. Serve boiling hot as a shared stew with rice.

Ch'unch'ŏn tak kalbi: Ch'unch'ŏn-style Chicken

This filling and spicy chicken dish is a specialty of Ch'unch'ŏn, a city in Kangwŏn Province. It is traditionally made with a whole chicken cut up into pieces, but the following recipe uses boneless, skinless chicken for an easier to enjoy and healthier meal. The ingredients reflect the changing nature of Korean cuisine as new ingredients are being incorporated into cooking, such as curry powder and 'western' cabbage (*yang paech'u*).

Serves 2–3

Ingredients
350g boneless chicken, cut into small, bite-sized pieces
5 tbsp cooking oil

Seasoning
2 tbsp *koch'ujang*
2 tbsp *soju* (or dry wine)
1 tbsp brown sugar
3 cloves crushed garlic
½ tbsp malt syrup (Korean-style malt syrup is available in Korean or Asian markets)
½ tbsp oyster sauce
½ tbsp soy sauce
1 tbsp fine chilli powder

⅓ tbsp curry powder
⅓ tbsp powdered ginger powder
a pinch of black pepper
⅓ tbsp roasted sesame seeds

Vegetables
1 cup cabbage, cut into bite-sized pieces
½ cup spring onions, cut into 3cm lengths
1 medium onion, chopped finely

Combine all the seasonings with the chicken and knead in well. Allow the mixture to marinate for 30 minutes. Heat the cooking oil in a large frying pan and when hot, add the chicken followed by the yellow onion, cabbage and green onions. Cook the mixture until done, stirring occasionally. Serve as a shared dish with rice.

Pudae tchigae: Military Camp Stew

Not a 'traditional' food by any means, but a popular choice nowadays. Just about anything goes when making this stew, so feel free to be creative and substitute to make your own rendition. This is also a very simple dish to prepare.

Serves 4

Ingredients
1.2 litres anchovy stock (see the *kkotge t'ang* recipe above for instructions)
½ cup sour (*paech'u*) *kimch'i*
½ cup Spam (or similar canned meat) (around half a tin)
1 cup sausage (or 1 ½ hot dogs)
½ cup chopped uncooked pork
2 tbsp tinned baked beans
½ cup enoki mushrooms (*p'aengi pŏsŏt*)
½ cup white rice cake ovals
½ pack ramen noodles (just noodles, not the soup base)
3 spring onions, cut into roughly 5cm lengths
2 sliced green chillies
2 sliced red chillies

2 tbsp Korean fine chilli pepper powder
1 tbsp soy sauce
1 tbsp *soju* (or dry wine)
1 ½ cloves crushed garlic
⅓ tbsp powdered ginger
black pepper to taste

Add all the above ingredients in a low flat pan and bring to a boil. This is best done on a tabletop burner. When the pork is done, it is ready to eat as a shared stew. Each diner can ladle some of the stew into an individual bowl to make eating easier. The ramen noodles should be eaten relatively quickly or else they will become overcooked and lose their flavour. Other recipes call for adding a slice or two of processed American cheese, cubes of tofu or strips of fishcake.

Serve this with rice and fresh carrot or cucumber sticks (dipped in *toenjang* or *koch'ujang* directly before eating). *Soju* is a perfect drink to accompany this eclectic stew.

Side-dishes

Samsaek namul: Three-colour Vegetables

This dish is made by preparing three different kinds of vegetables separately, and then serving them all on one dish.

Serves 3–4

1. Spinach
Ingredients
300g spinach, washed and roots removed
½ tbsp salt
1 tbsp soy sauce
1 tbsp spring onions
6 cloves crushed garlic
½ tbsp sesame oil
½ tbsp crushed, roasted sesame seeds

Fill a large saucepan with water, add salt and bring to a roaring boil. Add the spinach and blanch for 30 seconds; remove and rinse in cold water. Squeeze the excess water out of the spinach and then mix with the other ingredients.

2. Fernbrake
Ingredients
300g fernbrake
1 tbsp soy sauce
½–1 clove crushed garlic
vegetable oil for stir-frying
250ml water
1 tbsp crushed, roasted sesame seeds
½ tbsp sesame oil
pinch of black pepper

Soak the dried fernbrake in water overnight so that it is soft. Drain the fernbrake and cut any hard parts off and discard. Cut the remaining fernbrake into roughly 5 cm lengths. Mix the drained and cut fernbrake with the soy sauce and crushed garlic and let stand for 15 minutes.

Next, heat oil in a large frying-pan, add the fernbrake and fry it for a few minutes; add the water to the frying-pan and cover. When done, remove from the pan and mix with the remaining ingredients.

3. Mung bean sprouts
Ingredients
200g mung bean sprouts – 200 grams
½ tbsp salt
½ tbsp soy sauce
½–1 cloves crushed garlic
½ tbsp sesame oil
½ tbsp crushed, roasted sesame seeds

Wash the bean sprouts and parboil in boiling water for around 1 minute. Drain and rinse well before mixing with the other ingredients.

Arrange all three vegetables on the same dish and serve.

Kkaktugi: Radish kimch'i

While most types of *kimch'i* can be difficult to prepare correctly, *kkaktugi* is relatively simple for even a novice cook. When prepared at the royal palace, this type of *kimch'i* was known as *mu songsongi*.

> *Ingredients*
> 2 daikon radishes (around 2kg in total), cubed
> 3 tbsp coarse sea salt
> 2 tbsp chilli powder
> 4 spring onions, cut into 4cm lengths
> 1 tbsp anchovy sauce
> 1 tbsp sugar
> ½–1 cloves crushed garlic
> 1 tsp powdered ginger

Put the daikon radish in a large mixing bowl and sprinkle with the salt. Allow this to sit for about 30 minutes, after which time any water that appears should be drained off.

Next, add the chilli powder and mix together. The remaining ingredients can then be mixed in. The entire mixture should then be put into a jar and sealed; after one day at room temperature the *kkaktugi* is ready to eat.

Keep refrigerated.

Manŭl changatchi: Pickled Whole Garlic

This is a very healthy and easy to make side-dish that complements nearly any Korean meal well. The pickled garlic has a tangy, but not overly strong, flavour.

> *Ingredients*
> 40 cloves of peeled garlic
>
> First liquid mixture
> 480 ml cool water
> 5 tbsp coarse salt

Second liquid mixture
240 ml water
240 brown rice vinegar
3 tbsp coarse salt
4 tbsp soy sauce

Put the garlic cloves in a sterile 0.5 litre liddled jar. Dissolve 5 table-spoons of coarse salt in two cups water and add this to the garlic; seal the jar and allow the mixture to sit at room temperature for one week.

Drain the liquid and discard. Next, bring the water, vinegar (brown rice vinegar is bast), coarse salt and soy sauce to a boil in a small saucepan and leave to cool. Add this to the jar with the garlic, seal the jar and put it in a cool place.

After one day, remove the garlic and bring the liquid to a boil. After cooling, add to the garlic again.

Then, after another two days, repeat this process of boiling; when the water has cooled, add the garlic and refrigerate. The pickled garlic is now ready to enjoy as a side-dish.

Pibim pap: Rice Mixed with Vegetables

This dish is likely to have been originally developed by peasants, but it is now very much a representative food of Korea. What one can add to this dish is really only limited by imagination and availability of ingredients, so feel free to substitute ingredients with whatever might be on hand, especially seasonal foods – this is truly in keeping with the spirit of this dish. For example, in the summer *pibim pap* makes a refreshing and fill-ing dish – with very little preparation time – when prepared with uncooked ingredients such as fresh lettuce leaves, thinly sliced cucumber and carrot and crown daisy (*ssukk'at*) served over brown rice with a good amount of *koch'ujang*. *Pibim pap* can also be prepared with or without meat and with either white rice or brown rice.

For preparing spinach, mung bean sprouts and fernbrake, follow the directions under *Samsaek namul*: Three-colour Vegetables above. Add about $\frac{1}{4}$ cup of each prepared vegetable to each bowl of *pibim pap*.

Serves 2

Ingredients
100g shredded beef
1 tbsp soy sauce
1 tbsp sesame oil
½ tbsp sugar
1 tbsp sesame oil
3 dried shitake mushrooms (soak in water to soften and then remove stems and slice)
½ cup carrots, julienned
½ cup cucumber, julienned
¼ cup prepared spinach
¼ cup prepared mung bean sprouts
¼ cup prepared fernbrake

2 fried eggs, one for each bowl
red pepper paste to taste

Stir-fry the beef with the sesame oil, soy sauce and sugar – cook thoroughly, but do not overcook. Next heat the second quantity of sesame oil and stir-fry the mushrooms, carrots and cucumber, in that order. Add cooked rice to two large bowls and top with the beef, spinach, mung bean sprouts, fernbrake, mushrooms, carrots and cucumber. Place a fried egg on top and serve. Add *koch'ujang* paste to taste and mix well before eating.

For other variations, substitute the beef with imitation crab, add chopped *kimch'i* to the bowls to give the rice even more spice, or add roasted, crumbled laver. There is no wrong way to enjoy *pibim pap*.

Mu saengch'ae: Daikon Radish Salad

This is a vegetable dish served at the royal palace in past times and is easy to prepare. It can be made with or without the chilli powder.

Ingredients
300g daikon radish
2 tsp chilli powder
1 tbsp salt
1 tbsp brown sugar

1 tbsp vinegar
1 chopped spring onion
½–1 clove crushed garlic
½ tsp crushed ginger (around 1cm)
1 tsp sesame oil
1 tsp roasted sesame seeds

Peel the daikon radish and cut into very thin strips of about 5cm in length. Add the remaining ingredients and mix thoroughly. If desired, separate the radish into two bowls and add the chilli powder to only one, creating one dish of spicy radish and one that is mild.

Oi saengch'ae: Spicy Cucumber Salad

This dish is similar to the above, but uses sliced cucumber.

Ingredients
1 large cucumber, about 450 grams
1 tbsp coarse sea salt
1 tbsp Korean fine chilli pepper powder
1 tbsp brown sugar
1 tbsp sesame oil
1 tbsp salt
1 tbsp vinegar
½–1 cloves crushed garlic
½ tbsp roasted sesame seeds

Cut both ends off the cucumber and slice into thin rounds. In a large bowl, add the cucumber and salt, and mix. After 30 minutes quickly rinse the cucumber and squeeze out any water. Add the seasonings and mix well.

Piji tchigae: Soy Bean-curd Stew

The English name of this stew might not sound appetizing, but once you try this hearty dish your opinion will change.

Serves 2

Ingredients
½ cups anchovy stock (see the *kkotge t'ang* recipe above for instructions)
½ cup sour *kimch'i* (*paech'u kimch'i*)
½ cup pork (boneless)
6 tbsp *kimch'i* juice (the liquid from the *kimch'i* jar)
½ cup soy beans
60 ml water
½ tbsp soy sauce

The soybeans should be soaked overnight before cooking so they are soft. Remove any bean skins before grinding. To grind, add 60 ml water to ½ cup soybeans, and using a good quality blender make a thick, white paste of the beans and water. The ground soybean curd is known as *piji*.

Bring the anchovy stock to a boil and discard the anchovies and *tasima*. Add the *kimch'i*, uncooked pork and *kimch'i* juice to the pot and bring to a boil. Add the blended *piji* to the pot along with the soy sauce and boil. If the soup is a little bland, add more soy sauce. Serve as a shared side-dish along with rice.

Tubu chorim: Spicy Braised Tofu

This side-dish is a traditional part of vegetarian Buddhist temple fare and provides a good source of protein. The spiciness of the tofu can be regulated by the amount of chilli powder and chillies used as seasoning.

Ingredients
2 tbsp cooking oil
210g firm tofu (extra firm is even better), sliced into pieces about 1cm thick
2–3 chopped spring onions
3–4 tbsp soy sauce
½–1 clove crushed garlic
½ tbsp Korean fine chilli pepper powder
½ tbsp sesame oil
1 tbsp roasted sesame seeds
1 red or green chilli, finely chopped with seeds removed
2 tbsp water

Heat the oil in a large frying pan and when hot, place the tofu in the pan and cook at a medium heat. Mix the other ingredients together and when the tofu is golden brown on both sides, spoon the sauce on the tofu and allow to cook for another minute or so at a very low heat.

Tubu kimch'i: Tofu with *Kimch'i*

This is another dish using tofu that is commonly served as a side-dish in drinking houses. Easy to prepare, it is also very tasty and nutritious.

Ingredients
420g firm (or extra firm) tofu (1 block), sliced into pieces about 1cm thick
300g sliced cabbage (*paech'u*) *kimch'i*
150g sliced pork belly, cut very thinly and in bite-sized pieces
1–2 cloves crushed garlic
2 chopped spring onions
1 tbsp sesame oil
½ tbsp brown sugar
1 tbsp roasted sesame seeds

Heat a small amount of cooking oil in a frying pan and add the *kimch'i*, pork, garlic and green onions and stir-fry until the pork is completely cooked (about 4 minutes). Turn off the heat and mix in the sesame oil and seeds.

Bring water in a medium saucepan to a full boil and put the pieces of tofu in the water for about 20 seconds each before removing and draining. This task is made easier if the tofu is placed in a colander or sieve before putting in the water. Arrange the *kimch'i* and pork mixture in the centre of a plate and place the tofu in a ring around the plate's edge. Sprinkle with roasted sesame seeds and serve.

Haemul p'ajŏn: Seafood Pancakes

A popular dish in drinking houses, this can be prepared with almost any type of seafood such as oysters, clams or squid. It is best enjoyed with *makkŏlli* or similar rice wine.

Ingredients
40g glutinous rice flour
40g wheat flour
1 tsp salt
1 tsp white pepper
1 egg, beaten
100g shucked fresh oysters
3 or 4 spring onions, cut into 3cm lengths
1 or 2 unseeded red chillies, sliced in thin strips
3–4 tbsp vegetable oil

Mix the flours, salt, pepper and egg with water to make a smooth and fairly thin batter that can be poured. Add the spring onions and oysters and set aside.

Heat the cooking oil in a large frying-pan and when hot, ladle in a thin layer of the mixture to make a pancake. Cook until browned underneath and set on the top (about 3 minutes), and then turn over until it is a light brown colour. Cut the large pancake into bite-sized pieces and directly before eating dip into soy sauce.

Other seafood can be substituted or added to the above recipe, such as sliced squid or shelled shrimp.

Drinks

Makkŏlli: Rice Wine

This is the simplest of all Korean drinks and probably the oldest too. The finished product can be enjoyed by either pouring the mixture through a sieve or ladling the liquid off the top of the jar – that part has the best taste and should be slightly sweet (do not drink the dregs on the bottom of the jar). After it is fully fermented, *makkŏlli* will keep longer if refrigerated. The colour of the finished *makkŏlli* will vary depending upon the yeast you use and the alcohol content will be significantly higher than the *makkŏlli* sold in stores, at around 15 percent.

1 kg white rice

200g *nuruk*, Korean yeast: if not available, use brewer's yeast
or malt

about 1.6 litres of fresh, room temperature water

As with all brewed liquors, sanitation of all utensils and containers is very important, so sterilize everything beforehand.

Steam the rice until cooked and then allow it to dry. Add the yeast to the rice and mix well. Next add water, approximately in a ratio of 5:6, yeast and rice:water, and mix well. Put the entire mixture into an earthenware pot (or other suitable container), cover and place in a warm area for 7 to 10 days.

To maintain a consistent temperature, wrap the fermentation container with towels or a blanket. Fermentation will cause the mixture to bubble slightly.

References

Throughout this work, Korean words are transliterated into English using the McCune-Reischauer system and Chinese words by the Pinyin system.

All translations are the author's own, except where otherwise indicated.

Introduction

1 Angus Hamilton, *Korea* (New York, 1904), p. 126.
2 Elizabeth Rozin, 'The Structure of Cuisine', in *The Psychobiology of Human Food Selection*, ed. L. M. Barker (Westport, CN, 1982); quoted in Katharine Milton, 'Food and Diet', in *Encyclopedia of Cultural Anthropology*, eds. David Levinson and Melvin Ember (New York, 1996) II, pp. 503–8, at p. 505.
3 Milton, 'Food and Diet', II, p. 506.
4 For the early history of Korea, see Ki-baik Lee, *A New History of Korea*, trans. Edward W. Wagner with Edward J. Shultz (Cambridge, MA, 1984), pp. 1–8.
5 Among the earliest records of polities on and around the Korean peninsula are those in the *Shiji* ('Records of the Historian'), *Han shu* ('History of the Former Han Dynasty') and *Sanguo zhi* ('History of the Three Kingdoms').
6 Recorded in the *Samguk yusa* ('Memorabilia of the Three Kingdoms') compiled by the monk Iryŏn around 1283.
7 Ki-baik Lee, *A New History of Korea*, pp. 26–7.
8 Ibid., pp. 14–15.
9 Han'guk chŏngsin munhwa yŏn'guwŏn, ed., *Chŏlla namdo ŭi hyangt'o*

munhwa ('The Regional Culture of South Chŏlla Province') (Sŏngnam, Korea, 2002), II, pp. 606–10.

10 See Jeon Sang-woon, *A History of Science in Korea* (Seoul, 1998), pp. 137–42.

11 Transplanting rice seedlings had been practiced on the Korean peninsula since the Three Kingdoms Period, but did not become general practice until the nineteenth century. See Yi Hyoji, *Han'guk ŭi ŭmsik munhwa* ('The Food Culture of Korea') (Seoul, 2006), p. 36.

12 Ki-baik Lee, *A New History of Korea*, pp. 226–7.

13 Ibid., pp. 347–8.

14 Yi Hyoji, *Han'guk ŭi ŭmsik munhwa*, pp. 44–5.

15 The tidal basins in Korea rank among the five largest in the world, along with those of eastern Canada, eastern United States, the North Sea coastline and the mouth of the Amazon River. See Kim Woong-seo, 'Korean Waters Abound with Marine Life', *Koreana* 20 (Summer 2006), pp. 20–5, at p. 24.

1 Daily Foods

1 Cho Sin, *Somun swoerok* ('Insignificant Records by Somun') in *P'aerim* ('Forest of Tales') (Seoul, 1969), p. 2, §25a.

2 Yun Sŏndo (1587–1671). Recorded in Chŏng Pyŏnguk, ed., *Sijo munhak sajŏn* ('Encyclopedia of *Sijo* Literature') (Seoul, 1980), p. 346, no. 1469.

3 Yi Kyubo, 'Tongmyŏng-wang p'yŏn' ('The lay of King Tongmyŏng'), in *Tongguk Yi Sangguk chip* [The Collected Works of Minister Yi of the Eastern Country [i.e., Korea]') (Seoul, 1982), 3, pp. 1–9.

4 The foundation dates for T'amna are not known; however, records indicate it was engaging with other Korean kingdoms by at least the fifth century. The myth entitled the 'Samsŏng sinhwa' ('Myth of the Three Surnames') is the foundation myth of T'amna, the island kingdom located on Cheju Island, and recorded in a fifteenth-century history. See *Koryŏsa* ('The History of the Koryŏ Dynasty') (Seoul, 1990), p. 57, 53b–54b.

5 Some scholars contend that varieties of millet have been cultivated on the Korean peninsula for over 5,000 years. See, Yun Sŏsŏk et al., *Han'guk minsok ŭi segye* ('Survey of Korean Folk Culture') (Seoul, 2001), III, p. 322.

6   See *Han'guk minjok munhwa taebaekkwa sajŏn* ('Encyclopaedia of Korean Culture'), 28 vols (Sŏngnam, 1994), XIV, pp. 226–34.

7   Yi Kyubo, *Tongguk Yi Sangguk chip*, appendix, p. 1, §3a.

8   Zhang Ying, *Panyou shier heshuo* ('Tales of Twelve Meals'), quoted in *Han'guk minjok munhwa taebaekkwa sajŏn* ('Encyclopedia of Korean Culture'), 28 vols (Sŏngnam, 1994), XIV, 226–34.

9   Sŏ Yugu, *Imwŏn kyŏngje simnyuk chi* ('Sixteen Treatises on Economy Written in Retirement'), quoted in Yun Sŏsŏk et al., *Han'guk minsok ŭi segye*, III, p. 338.

10 There are numerous records concerning barley including one for Silla in 114 CE stating that due to hail, the barley was damaged in the third lunar month; for Koguryŏ, we can find a record stating that the barley was damaged by frost in the fourth lunar month of 272 CE. See Kim Pusik, *Samguk sagi* ('History of the Three Kingdoms'), trans. Yi Pyŏngdo (Seoul, 1996), I, pp. 33, 399.

11 Iryŏn, *Samguk yusa* ('Memorabilia of the Three Kingdoms'), trans. Yi Minsu (Seoul, 1994), pp. 103–4.

12 *Kimun ch'onghwa* ('Collection of Tales Heard'), trans. Kim Tonguk (Seoul, 1996), I, pp. 310–11.

13 Yi Pinghŏhak, *Kyuhap ch'ongsŏ* ('Encyclopedia for Women's Daily Life'), (P'aju, Korea, 2006), p. 42.

14 Sŏ Yugu, *Chŭngbo sallim kyŏngje* ('Farm Management, Supplemented and Enlarged'), quoted in Yun Sŏsŏk et al., *Han'guk minsok ŭi segye*, III, p. 342.

15 Kim Pusik, *Samguk sagi* ('History of the Three Kingdoms') trans. into Modern Korean Yi Pyŏngdo (Seoul, 1996), I, p. 201.

16 Yi's literary collection is entitled *Mogŭn-jip* ('Collected Writings of Mogŭn') after his pen name, Mogŭn. Yi was one of the leading Confucian literati of the late Koryŏ period and is appraised as one of the exemplary literary talents of the Koryŏ dynasty.

17 *Sejong sillok* ('Veritable Records of King Sejong'), p. 66, 27b–28a (1434-12-24).

18 *Hyŏnjong sillok* ('Veritable Records of King Hyŏnjong') (1663), quoted in *Han'guk minjok munhwa taebaekkwa sajŏn*, II, p. 358.

19 Isabella Bird Bishop, *Korea and Her Neighbors* (Seoul, 1997 (first published 1898)), p. 155.

20 Sŏ Yugŏ, *Chŭngbo sallim kyŏngje*. quoted in Yun Sŏsŏk et al., *Han'guk minsok ŭi segye*, III, p. 364.

21 Yi Pinghŏhak, *Kyuhap ch'ongsŏ* ('Encyclopedia of Women's Daily

Life') annotated and trans. into Modern Korean Chŏng Ryangwan (P'ayu, 2006), p. 33.

22 For example, *Sallim kyŏngje* ('Farm Management') alone offers some twenty-five variations on *kanjang*.

23 Yi Sugwang, *Chibong yusŏl* ('Topical Discourses by Chibong') (Seoul, 1970), p. 20, 10b.

24 Oftentimes the Five Phases is interpreted as the 'Five Elements,' but this is not a theory of chemicals but rather a 'theory of metaphysics as a process.' See Keith Pratt and Richard Rutt, *Korea: A Historical and Cultural Dictionary* (Richmond, 1999), pp. 123–4.

25 Yi Sugwang, *Chibong yusŏl*, p. 19, §34a.

26 The radishes referred to here and elsewhere are *daikon* radishes, an elongated white radish.

27 There is an account in the Chinese history entitled the *Sanguo zhi* ('History of the Three Kingdoms') that states that the people of Koguryŏ excelled in making various fermented foodstuffs. See *Sanguo zhi, Dongyi chuan* ('History of the Three Kingdoms, Records of the Eastern Barbarians'), xxx.

28 Yi Kyubo, *Tongguk Yi Sangguk chip*, appendix, p. 4, 14a–14b.

29 Sŏ Kŏjŏng, *T'aep'yŏng hanhwa kolgye-jŏn* ('Idle Talk in a Peaceful Era'), trans. Pak Kyŏngsin (Seoul, 1998), II, pp. 47–8.

30 Yu Hŭich'un (1513–1577), recorded in Chŏng Pyŏnguk, ed., *Sijo munhak sajŏn* ('Encyclopedia of *Sijo* Literature') (Seoul, 1980), p. 199, no. 816.

31 'Tŭlnamul k'ae norae,' quoted in *Han'guk minjok munhwa taebaekkwa sajŏn*, V, p. 207.

32 Yi Ik, *Sŏngho sasŏl* ('Insignificant Explanations by Sŏngho'), quoted in Yun Sŏsŏk *et al.*, *Han'guk minsok ŭi segye*, III, p. 353.

33 Sŏ Kŏjŏng, *T'aep'yŏng hanhwa kolgye-jŏn*, I, p. 588.

34 In pre-modern Korea and much of East Asia, the calendar was based upon the two systems of ancient Chinese characters for dates: the Ten Heavenly Stems for the days of the ten-day week and the Twelve Earthly Branches for the twelve moons of the year. The characters used for the Heavenly Stems were matched with colours and those for the Earthly Branches indicated certain animals. Thus, 'cow' day was the first day of the lunar New Year in which the Earthly Branch was the character for 'cow.' See Keith Pratt and Richard Rutt, *Korea: A Historical and Cultural Dictionary* (Richmond, 1999), pp. 199–202.

35 Yi Sugwang, *Chibong yusŏl*, p. 19, 32a.
36 Kim Pusik, *Samguk sagi*, I, p. 28.
37 Xu Jing, *Gaoli tujing* ('Illustrated Account of Koryŏ') (Seoul, 2000), p. 23, 2a.
38 Recorded in *Ch'ŏnggu yŏngŏn*, *Haedong kayo* ('Songs of the Green Hills, Songs of the Eastern Country') in *Taedang yasŭng* ('Tales of the Eastern country') (Seoul, 1974), pp. 172–3.
39 O Sukkwŏn, *P'aegwan chapki* ('A Storyteller's Miscellany') (Seoul, 1971), pp. 538–9, 778–9.

2 Ritual and Seasonal Foods

1 Recorded in *Han'guk yŏryu hansi-sŏn* ('Anthology of *Hansi* Poetry by Korean Women'), ed. Chu Tuhyŏn (Seoul, Tŏaehaksa, 1994), p. 90. Hŏ Nansŏrhŏn is acclaimed as one of the greatest women poets of the Chosŏn period and her poems were even published in China.
2 See Zhen Shou, *Sanguo zhi* ('History of the Three Kingdoms') (Beijing, 1973), p. 841.
3 Hŏ Chun, *Tongŭi pogam* ('Exemplar of Eastern [i.e., Korean] Medicine'), ed. Kugyŏk Wiwŏnhoe (Seoul, 1966), 'Chappyŏng-p'yŏn 4' ('Section on Various Diseases, 4'), p. 428.
4 Lady Song (fl. mid-sixteenth century), recorded in *Han'guk yŏryu hansi-sŏn*, p. 234.
5 Chŏng Yagyong, *Yŏyudang chŏnsŏ* ('Writings by Yŏyudang') (Sŏngnam, 1999), p. 3, 11a.
6 *Koryŏsa* ('The History of the Koryŏ Dynasty') (Seoul, 1990), p. 16, 16a–b.
7 Kim Hyesung, *Manbŏp kyŏngjŏn* ('The Complete Scriptures') (Seoul, 1994), pp. 69–70. For a brief description of preparations for shamanic rites in English, see Michael J. Pettid, 'From Abandoned Daughter to Shaman Matriarch: An Analysis of the "Pari kongju muga", A Korean Shamanistic Song', PhD diss. (University of Hawaii, 1999), pp. 174–85.
8 Chŏng Hagyu, 'Nongga wŏlmyŏng-ga' ('Song of the Farmer's Calendar'), recorded in Im Kijung, ed., *Chosŏnjo ŭi kasa* ('The *kasa* Poems of the Chosŏn dynasty') (Seoul, 1989), p. 203.
9 Yi Sugwang, *Chibong yusŏl* ('Topical Discourses by Chibong') (Seoul, 1970), p. 19, 32b–33a.
10 Ibid.

11 Hong Sŏgmu, *Tongguk sesigi* ('Seasonal Customs of the Eastern Country' (i.e. Korea)), trans. Kang Muhak (Seoul, 1990), pp. 178–9.

12 Recorded in *Han'guk minsok taesajŏn* ('Encyclopedia of Korean Folk Culture') (Seoul, 1991), p. 1, 435.

13 Napp'yŏng Day falls on the third 'sheep' day after the winter solstice. On this day hunted meat was offered at rites held at the royal ancestral shrine among other places.

14 Chŏng Hagyu, 'Nongga wŏlmyŏng-ga', p. 204.

3 Regional Specialities

1 Yi Sugwang, *Chibong yusŏl* ('Topical Discourses by Chibong') (Seoul, 1970), p. 19, 43b.

2 Ki-baik Lee, *A New History of Korea*, trans. Edward W. Wagner with Edward J. Shultz (Cambridge, MA, 1984), p. 80.

3 This work was later incorporated into the dynastic records as the *Sejong sillok chiri chi* (Seoul, 1958), vols 148–55.

4 See *Chŏlla namdo ŭi hyangt'o munhwa* ('The Local Culture of South Chŏlla Province') (Sŏngnam, Korea, 2002), pp. 612–15.

5 Kim Pusik, *Samguk sagi* ('History of the Three Kingdoms'), trans. Yi Pyŏngdo (Seoul, 1996), II, pp. 69–70.

4 Drinks

1 This is the eighth and final verse of a poem song by an anonymous composer of the late Koryŏ period. Recorded in Pak Pyŏngch'ae, *Koryŏ kayo ŭi ŏsŏk yŏn'gu* ('A Study of the Terminology in Koryŏ-period Songs') (Seoul, 1994), pp. 214–43.

2 Yi Sugwang, *Chibong yusŏl* ('Topical Discourses by Chibong') (Seoul, 1970), p. 19, 34b.

3 Kim Pusik, *Samguk sagi* ('History of the Three Kingdoms'), trans. Yi Pyŏngdo (Seoul, 1996), II, p. 348.

4 Kim Kyŏnghun, *Ttŭtpakkŭi ŭmsiksa* ('An Unexpected History of Food') (Seoul, 2006), pp. 223–4.

5 Hwang Hŭi (1363–1452), recorded in Chŏng Pyŏnguk, ed., *Sijo munhak sajŏn* ('Encyclopedia of *Sijo* Literature') (Seoul, 1980), p. 636, no. 156.

6 Dwight B. Heath, 'Alcohol and Drugs,' in *Encyclopedia of Cultural*

Anthropology, eds. David Levinson and Melvin Ember (New York, 1996), I, p. 39.

7 Recorded in Yi Kyubo, 'Tongmyŏng-wang p'yŏn' ('The Lay of King Tongmyŏng'), in *Tongguk Yi Sangguk chip* ('The Collected Works of Minister Yi of the Eastern Country ('i.e., Korea') (Seoul, 1982) III, pp. 31–9.

8 Xu Jing, *Gaoli tujing* ('Illustrated account of Koryŏ') (Seoul, 2000), p. 26, 2a–2b.

9 Recorded in Chŏng Pyŏnguk, ed., *Sijo munhak sajŏn* ('Encyclopedia of *Sijo* Literature') (Seoul, 1980), p. 421, no. 1811.

10 *Omija* is the fruit of the Maximowiczia chinensis tree, which is found in Korea, Japan, Manchuria and northern China. The name means the 'five tastes': that is, sweet, sour, bitter, salty and spicy.

11 Liu Ling (fl. 3rd cent. CE) and Tao Qian were two famous Chinese poets who were said to have a great love for wine.

12 Recorded in Chŏng Pyŏnguk, *Han'guk kojŏn siga-ron* ('Treatise on Pre-modern Korean Poem-songs') (Seoul, 2000), p. 417.

13 *Han'guk minsok taesajŏn* ('Encyclopedia of Korean folk culture'), (Seoul, 1991), II, p. 909. Prohibitions on alcohol seem to have occurred in both Koryŏ and Chosŏn. The earliest ban in Koryŏ was in 1021 and was based on Buddhist prohibitions against intoxicants, while those in Chosŏn seem mostly related to the over-consumption of rice by commoners in making alcoholic drinks. None of the bans seem to have lasted particularly long, given the regularity of subsequent bans. See Chŏng Taesŏng, *Uri sul ŭi yŏksa wa munhwa kŭrigo chihye* ('The History and Culture of our Liquor, and Wisdom') (Seoul, 2006), pp. 162–4.

14 *Sŏngjong sillok* ('Veritable Records of King Sŏnjong'), p. 239, 4b–5a (1490-04-10).

15 Yi Sugwang, *Chibong yusŏl*, p. 19, §38a.

16 Xu Jing, *Gaoli tujing*, p. 22, 3a.

17 Sŏ Kŏjŏng, *T'aep'yŏng hanhwa kolgye-jŏn* ('Idle Talk in a Peaceful Era'), trans. Pak Kyŏngsin (Seoul, 1998), I, pp. 356–8.

18 Kim Pusik, *Samguk sagi*, I, p. 267.

19 Iryŏn, *Samguk yusa* ('Memorabilia of the Three Kingdoms'), trans. Yi Minsu (Seoul, 1994), p. 220.

20 Suk Yong-un, 'History and Philosophy of Korean Tea Art', *Koreana* 11 (Winter 1997), p. 7.

21 *Koryŏsa* ('The History of the Koryŏ Dynasty') (Seoul, 1990), p. 69, §5a.

22 Ŭisan, *Ch'oŭi sŏnjip* ('Anthology of Ch'oŭi') (Seoul, 1977), II, 827.

23 Mentioned above, *omija* is the fruit of the Maximowiczia chinensis tree.

24 The summary of medical qualities of these teas is based in part on Yu Tae-jong, 'Teas and their Medicinal Effects', *Koreana* 11 (Winter 1997), pp. 28–33.

5 Foods of the Royal Palace

1 *Unyŏng-jŏn* ('The Tale of Unyŏng'), handwritten unpublished manuscript, p. 42.

2 Ki-baik Lee, *A New History of Korea*, trans. Edward W. Wagner with Edward J. Shultz (Cambridge, MA, 1984), p. 78.

3 Iryŏn, *Samguk yusa* ('Memorabilia of the Three Kingdoms'), trans. Yi Minsu (Seoul, 1994), p. 145.

4 See Han Pongnyŏ and Chŏng Kilja, *Chosŏn wangjo kungjung ŭmsik* ('The Palace Food of the Chosŏn Dynasty') (Seoul, 2006), p. 27.

5 Kim Yongsuk, *Chosŏnjo kungjung p'ungsok yŏn'gu* ('A Study of the Palace Customs of the Chosŏn Dynasty') (Seoul, 1987), pp. 18–19.

6 See Han Pongnyŏ and Chŏng Kilja, *Chosŏn wangjo kungjung ŭmsik*, pp. 49–53.

7 *Yŏngjo sillok* ('Veritable Records of King Yŏngjo'), quoted in Yun Sŏsŏk et al., *Han'guk minsok ŭi segye* ('Survey of Korean Folk Culture'), III, pp. 502–3. This comment was made by the king in the context of reducing the number of meals to three a day in an attempt to be frugal.

6 The Kitchen Space and Utensils

1 Yun Kukhyŏng, *Kapchin man-rŏk* ('Scattered Records from the *Kapchin* Year [i.e., 1604]') in *P'aeruin* ('Forest of Tales') (Seoul, 1969), 4b.

2 *Xin Tangshu Dongyi chuan* ('New History of Tang, Records of the Eastern Barbarians'), ed. Pang Kusong and Kim Chwasŏn (Seoul, 1996), pp. 179–94.

3 Iryŏn, *Samguk yusa* ('Memorabilia of the Three Kingdoms'), trans. Yi Minsu (Seoul, 1994), p. 494.

4 'Sangjŏ-ga'('Song of the Pestle'). Recorded in Pak Pyŏngch'ae, *Koryŏ kayo ŭi ŏsŏk yŏn'gu* ('A Study of the Terminology in Koryŏ

Period Songs') (Seoul, 1994), pp. 365–9. The refrains at the end of each line are onomatopoetic phrases designed to heighten the emotion of the song.

5 Yi Tŏngmu, *Sasojŏl* ('Elementary Etiquette for Scholar Families'), quoted in *Sources of Korean Tradition, Volume Two: From the Sixteenth to the Twentieth Centuries*, eds. Yŏngho Ch'oe, Peter H. Lee and W. Theodore deBary (New York, 2000), p. 62.

7 Food in Contemporary Korea

1 Leonard Lueras and Nedra Chung, eds, *Korea* (Hong Kong, 1981).
2 This data was obtained from the country handbook on South Korea published by the Library of Congress and available online at http://countrystudies.us/south-korea/ (accessed May 2007).
3 Yi Hyoji, *Han'guk ŭi ŭmsik munhwa* ('The Food Culture of Korea') (Seoul, 2006), p. 42.
4 Pak Ki-Hyuk with Sidney D. Gamble, *The Changing Korean Village* (Seoul, 1975), p. 104.
5 Yi Hyoji, *Han'guk ŭi ŭmsik munhwa*, p. 45.
6 Ibid., p. 47.
7 Vincent S. R. Brandt, *A Korean Village, Between Farm and Sea* (Cambridge, MA, 1971), pp. 50–51.
8 Yi Hyoji, *Han'guk ŭi ŭmsik munhwa*, p. 48.
9 This information is found on the website of the Intergovernmental Panel on Climate Change at http://www.grida.no/climate/ipcc_tar/wg2/435.htm (accessed May 2007).
10 This according to FAO and World Bank figures at http://www.ucpress.edu/books/pages/9577/pdf/Atlas.43-46.pdf (accessed May 2007).
11 Hŏ Chun, *Tongŭi pogam* ('Exemplar of Eastern [i.e., Korean] Medicine'), ed. Kugyŏk Wiwŏnhoe, 'Chappyŏng-p'yŏn 4' ('Section on Various Diseases, 4') (Seoul, 1966), p. 351.
12 All this and more according to the website for the Korean Agro-Fisheries Trade Corporation. See http://www.sauce.or.kr/eng/sybnpst/story/story_menu05.php (accessed September 2006).

Bibliography

Primary Sources

Chang-ssi, *Ŭmsik timibang* ('Recipes for Tasty Food'), ed. Yi Hoch'ŏl (Taegu, Korea, 2005)

Cho Sin, *Somun swoerok* ('Insignificant Records by Somun'), reproduction of original text, in *P'aerim* ('Forest of Tales') (Seoul, 1969)

Chŏng, Yagyong, *Yŏyudang chŏnsŏ* ('Writings by Yŏyudang'), reproduction of original text (Songnam, 1999)

Ch'ŏnggu yŏngŏn, Haedong kayo ('Songs of the Green Hills; Songs of the Eastern Country'), reproduction of original texts (Seoul, 1974)

Chosŏn wangjo sillok ('Veritable Records of the Chosŏn Dynasty') 48 vols, reproduction of original text (Seoul, 1958)

Hŏ Chun, *Tongŭi pogam* ('Exemplar of Eastern [i.e. Korean] Medicine'), ed. Kugyŏk Wiwŏnhoe (Seoul, 1966)

Hong Sŏgmu, *Tongguk sesigi* ('Seasonal Customs of the Eastern [i.e. Korea] Country'), trans. into modern Korean Kang Muhak (Seoul, 1990)

Iryŏn, *Samguk yusa* ('Memorabilia of the Three Kingdoms'), trans. into modern Korean Yi Minsu (Seoul, 1994)

Kim, Chŏngsŏ, et al. *Koryŏ sa chŏryo* ('Chronological Summary of Koryŏ'), reproduction of original text (Seoul, 1991)

Kim, Pusik, *Samguk sagi* ('History of the Three Kingdoms'), trans. into modern Korean Yi Pyŏngdo (Seoul, 1996)

Kimun ch'onghwa ('Collection of Tales Heard') 5 vols, trans. into modern Korean Kim Tonguk (Seoul, 1996)

Koryŏsa ('The History of the Koryŏ Dynasty'), reproduction of original text (Seoul, 1990)

Kungjung kwan-hon cherye ('Wedding and Capping Ceremonies of the Royal Palace'), reproduction of original text (Seoul, 1996)

No, Sasin, *et al.*, *Sinjŭng Tongguk yŏji sŭngnam* ('Newly Enlarged Geographical Survey of the Eastern Country'), reproduction of original text (Seoul, 1994)

O Sukkwŏn, *P'aegwan chapki* ('A Storyteller's Miscellany'), in *Taedong yasŭng* ('Tales of the Eastern Country') (Seoul, 1971)

Sŏ Kŏjŏng, *P'ilwŏn chapki* ('Writing Brush Garden Miscellany') reproduction of original text, in *Taedong yasŭng* ('Tales of the Eastern Country') (Seoul, 1971)

—, *T'aep'yŏng hanhwa kolgye-jŏn* ('Idle Talk in a Peaceful Era'), trans. into modern Korean Pak Kyŏngsin (Seoul, 1998)

Sŏ Yugu, *Imwŏn simnyuk chi* ('Sixteen Treatises Written in Retirement') reproduction of original text (Seoul, 1966)

Sŏng, Hyŏn, *Yongjae ch'onghwa* ('Assorted Writings by Yongjae'), reproduction of original text (Seoul, 2000)

Taedong kimun ('Strange Tales of the East'), reproduction of original text (Seoul, 1995)

Tongp'ae raksong ('Oft-recited Tales of the Eastern Country'), trans. into modern Korean Kim Tonguk (Seoul, 1996)

Ŭisan, *Ch'oŭi sŏnjip* ('Anthology of Ch'oŭi') (Seoul, 1977)

Unyŏng-jŏn ('The Tale of Unyŏng'), handwritten, unpublished manuscript

Xu, Jing, *Gaoli tujing* ('Illustrated Account of Koryŏ') reproduction of original text (Seoul, 2000)

Yi Chehyŏn, *Yŏgong p'aesŏl* ('Jottings by Yŏgong'), trans. into modern Korean Minjok munhwa ch'unjin-hoe (Seoul, 1997)

Yi Ik, *Sangho sasŏl* ('Insignificant explanations by Sŏngho'), trans. into modern Korean Minjok munhwa ch'unjin-hoe (Seoul, 1997)

Yi Kyubo, *Tongguk Yi Sangguk chip* ('Collected works of Minister Yi of the Eastern Country') reproduction of original text (Seoul, 1982)

Yi-ssi Pinghŏgak, *Kyuhap ch'ongsŏ* ('Encyclopedia of Women's Daily Life'), annotated and trans. into modern Korean Chŏng Ryangwan (P'aju, 2006)

Yi Sugwang, *Chibong yusŏl* ('Topical Discourses by Chibong') reproduction of original text (Seoul, 1970)

Yu Chungnim, *Sallim kyŏngje* ('Rural Economies'), trans. into modern Korean Minjok munhwa ch'unjin-hoe (Seoul, 1997)

Yun Kukhyŏng, *Kapchin man-rŏk* ('Scattered Records from the *Kapchin* Year [i.e., 1604]'), reproduction of original text, in *P'aerim* ('Forest of Tales') (Seoul, 1969)

Zhen Shou, *Sanguo zhi*, *Tongi-jŏn* ('History of the Three Kingdoms, Records of the Eastern Barbarians') (Beijing, 1973)

Secondary Sources

Bishop, Isabella Bird, *Korea and Her Neighbors*, first published 1898 (Seoul, 1997)

Brandt, Vincent S. R., *A Korean Village, Between the Farm and Sea* (Cambridge, MA, 1971)

Chang, Chugŭn, *P'ulŏssŭn Han'guk ŭi sinhwa* ('Korean Myths, Rewritten') (Seoul, 1998)

Chin, Sŏnggi, *Namguk ŭi minsok* ('Folk Customs of the Southern Country') (Seoul, 1978)

Ch'oe, Chŏngho, *San kwa Han'gugin ŭi sam* ('Mountains and the Lives of Koreans') (Seoul, 1993)

Ch'oe, Sangsu, *Annual Customs of Korea* (Seoul, 1960)

—, *Han'guk minsok nori ŭi yŏn'gu* ('A Study of Korean Folk Games') (Seoul, 1985)

Ch'oe, Pŏmsŏ, *Yasaro ponŭn Chosŏn ŭi yŏksa* ('Chosŏn History as Seen Through Unofficial Narratives'), 2 vols (Seoul, 2003)

Ch'oe, Sukkyŏng and Ha Hyŏngang, *Han'guk yŏsŏng sa: Kodae Chosŏn sidae* ('A History of Korean Women: From Ancient Times through the Chosŏn Period') (Seoul, 1993)

Ch'oe, Yŏngho, Peter H. Lee and W. Theodore deBary, eds, *Sources of Korean Tradition, Volume Two: From the Sixteenth to the Twentieth Centuries* (New York, 2000)

Chŏng Pyŏnguk, ed., *Sijo munhak sajŏn* ('Encyclopedia of *Sijo* Literature') (Seoul, 1980)

—, *Han'guk kojŏn siga-ron* ('Treatise on Pre-modern Korean Poemsongs') (Seoul, 2000)

Chŏng, Taesŏng, *Uri sul ŭi yŏksa wa munhwa kŭrigo chihye* ('The History and Culture of our Liquor, and Wisdom'), trans. into modern Korean Ch'oe Chinsŏn (Seoul, 2006)

Chu, Tuhyŏn, ed., *Han'guk yŏryu hansi-sŏn* ('Anthology of *Hansi* Poetry by Korean Women') (Seoul, T'aehaksa, 1994)

Chun, Hui-Jung, et al., *Traditional Korean Food* (Seoul, 2000)

Chung, Soon Young, *Korean Home Cooking* (Boston, MA, 2002)

Eckert, Carter J. et al., *Korea Old and New: A History* (Seoul, 1990)

Hamilton, Angus, *Korea* (New York, 1904)

Han, Chŏngsŏp, *Han'gugin ŭi minsok sinang* ('Folk Beliefs of Koreans') (Seoul, 1996)

Han, Pongnyŏ and Chŏng Kilja, *Chosŏn wangjo kungjung ŭmsik* ('The Palace Food of the Chosŏn Dynasty') (Seoul, 2006)

Han'guk chŏngsin munhwa yŏn'guwŏn, ed., *Han'gukhak kich'o charyo sŏnjip, kŭnse* ('Selected Basic Materials for Korean Studies, Modern Period'), 2 vols (Sŏngnam, 1994)

—, *Chŏlla namdo ŭi hyangt'o munhwa* ('The Regional Culture of South Chŏlla Province') (Sŏngnam, 2002)

Han'guk komunsŏ hakhoe, ed., *Chosŏn sidae saenghwalsa* ('The Daily Life History of the Chosŏn Dynasty') (Seoul, 2000)

—, *Chosŏn sidae saenghwalsa 2* ('The Daily Life History of the Chosŏn Dynasty, 2') (Seoul, 2002)

Han'guk minjok munhwa taebaekkwa sajŏn ('Encyclopedia of Korean Culture'), 28 vols (Sŏngnam, 1994)

Han'guk minsok taesajŏn ('Encyclopedia of Korean Folk Culture'), 2 vols (Seoul, 1991)

Han'guk munhwa sangjing sajŏn ('Encyclopedia of Korean Cultural Symbols'), 2 vols (Seoul, 1996)

Han'guk yŏksa yŏn'guhoe, ed., *Chosŏn sidae saramdŭl ŭn ŏttŏke sarassŭlkka* ('How did the People of Chosŏn Live?') (Seoul, 1996)

Heath, Dwight B., 'Alcohol and Drugs', in *Encyclopedia of Cultural Anthropology*, ed. David Levinson and Melvin Ember (New York, 1996)

Howard, Keith, *Bands, Songs, and Shamanistic Rituals: Folk Music in Korean Society* (Seoul, 1989)

Hoyt, James, *Soaring Phoenixes and Prancing Dragons: A Historical Survey of Korean Classical Literature* (Seoul, 2000)

Im, Kijung, ed. *Chosŏnjo ŭi kasa* ('The *Kasa* Poems of the Chosŏn Dynasty') (Seoul, 1989)

Im, Tonggwon, *Han'guk minsok munhwa ron* ('Treatise on Korean Folk Culture') (Seoul, 1983)

Jeon, Sang-woon, *A History of Science in Korea* (Seoul, 1998)

Kang, Inhŭi, *Han'gugin ŭi poyang sik* ('The Curative Foods of Koreans') (Seoul, 1992)

Kim, Hyesung, *Manbŏp kyŏngjŏn* ('The Complete Scriptures') (Seoul, 1994)

Kim, Hyŏnyŏng, et. al., *Chosŏn sidae sahoe ŭi mosŭp* ('The Shape of Society in the Chosŏn Period') (Seoul, 2003)

Kim, Kisuk and Han Kyŏngsŏn, *Ŭmsik kwa siksaenghwal munhwa* ('Food and Dietary Customs') (Seoul, 1997)

Kim, Kyŏnghun, *Ttŭtpakkŭi ŭmsiksa* ('An Unexpected History of Food') (Seoul, 2006)

Kim, Manjo, 'Kimchi', *Koreana* 11 (Autumn 1997)

Kim, Man-Jo, Lee Kyou-Tae, and Lee O-Young, *The Kimchee Cookbook: Fiery Flavors and Cultural History of Korea's National Dish* (London, 1999)

Kim, Pongok, *Cheju t'ongsa* ('A Complete History of Cheju') (Cheju City, 1990)

Kim, Sangbo, *Han'guk ŭi ŭmsik saenghwal munhwa sa* ('The History of Korean Food Culture') (Seoul, 1997)

Kim, Sŏkhyŏng, *Han'guksa wa nongmin* ('Korean History and Farmers') (Seoul, 1998)

Kim, Sŏngbae, *Han'guk ŭi minsok* ('Folk Customs of Korea') (Seoul, 1983)

Kim, T'aekkyu, 'Chosŏn hugi ŭi nonggyŏng ŭirye ŭi sesi' ('Agricultural Rites and Seasonal Customs in Late Chosŏn'), *Chŏngsin munhwa yŏn'gu* 16 (December, 1993)

Kim, Woong-seo, 'Korean Waters Abound with Marine Life', *Koreana* 20 (Summer 2006)

Kim, Yŏngdok, et al., *Han'guk yŏsŏngsa: Kaehwagi – 1945* ('A History of Korean Women: From the Enlightenment Period until 1945') (Seoul, 1993)

Kim, Yŏngdon, *Cheju-do Cheju saram* ('Cheju Island and Cheju People') (Seoul, 1999)

Kim, Yongsuk, *Chosŏnjo kungjung p'ungsok yŏn'gu* ('A Study of the Palace Customs in the Chosŏn Dynasty') (Seoul, 1987)

Kim, Yongt'ae, *Yet sallim yet munhwa iyagi* ('Stories of Life and Culture in Past Times') (Seoul, 1997)

Lee, Ki-baik, *A New History of Korea,* trans. Edward W. Wagner with Edward J. Shultz (Cambridge, MA, 1984)

Lueras, Leonard and Nedra Chung, eds, *Korea* (Hong Kong, 1981)

Milton, Katharine, 'Food and Diet', in *Encyclopedia of Cultural Anthropology*, ed. David Levinson and Melvin Ember (New York, 1996)

Moon, Okp'yo, *et al.*, *Chosŏn sidae kwan-hon-sang-che I, kwallye-hol-lye p'yŏn* ('The Ancestral, Funerary, Marriage and Capping Rites of the Chosŏn period, I, Capping and Marriage Rites volume' (Sŏngnam, 1999)

Pak, Ki-Hyuk with Sidney D. Gamble, *The Changing Korean Village* (Seoul, 1975)

Pak, Pyŏngch'ae, *Koryŏ kayo ŭi ŏsŏk yŏn'gu* ('A Study of the

Terminology in Koryŏ-period Songs') (Seoul, 1994)

Pang, Kusong and Kim Chwasŏn, eds, *Dongyi chuan* ('Records of the Eastern Barbarians') (Seoul, 1996)

Pettid, Michael J., 'From Abandoned Daughter to Shaman Matriarch: An Analysis of the "Pari kongju muga" a Korean Shamanistic Song', PhD diss. (University of Hawaii, 1999)

Pratt, Keith and Richard Rutt, *Korea: A Historical and Cultural Dictionary* (Richmond, 1999)

Sin, Myŏngho, *Kunggwŭl ŭi kkot: kungnyŏ* ('Flowers of the Palace: Palace Women') (Seoul, 2004)

Suk, Yong-un, 'History and Philosophy of Korean Tea Art', *Koreana* 11 (Winter 1997)

Wŏn, Yŏngsŏp, ed., *Uri soktam sajŏn* ('An Encyclopedia of our Proverbs') (Seoul, 1993)

Yi, Hyegyŏng, 'Kimch'i munhwa ŭi pyŏnchŏn-e kwanhan munhŏnjŏk koch'al' ('An Investigation of Documents Related to Changes in *kimch'i* Culture'), *Munhwajae* 23 (1990)

Yi, Hyoji, *Han'guk ŭi ŭmsik munhwa* ('The Food Culture of Korea') (Seoul, 2006)

Yi, Kiyŏl, *Han'gugin siksaenghwal ŭi yŏngyang p'yŏngga* ('A Nutritional Critique of Korean's Dietary Customs') (Seoul, 1996)

Yi, Kyut'ae, *Uri ŭi ŭmsik iyagi* ('Stories of our Food') (Seoul, 1991)

Yi, Myŏngbok, *Ch'ejirŭl almyŏn kŏngangi pointa* ('If One Understands the Physical Constitution, One Will See Good Health') (Seoul, 1993)

Yi, Songu, *Han'guk siksaenghwalsa yŏn'gu* ('A Study of the History of Korean Dietary Customs?') (Seoul, 1978)

—, *Chosŏn sidae chorisŏ ŭi punsŏkjŏk yŏn'gu* ('An Analytical Study of the Food Preparation Documents of the Chosŏn dynasty') (Sŏngnam, 1982)

Yu, Tae-jong, *Ŭmsik kunghap* ('Harmony of Foods') (Seoul, 1995)

—, 'Teas and their Medicinal Effects', *Koreana* 11 (Winter 1997)

Yun, Sŏsŏk, *Han'guk ŭi ŭmsik yongŏ* ('Terminology in Korean Food') (Seoul, 1991)

—, *Han'guk sikp'umsa yŏn'gu* ('A Study of Korean Foodstuffs') (Seoul, 1993)

Yun, Sŏsŏk, et al., *Han'guk minsok ŭi segye* ('Survey of Korean Folk Culture') vol. III (Seoul, 2001)

Acknowledgements

An undertaking like the present volume is not possible without the help and support of many individuals. In truth, this volume is the cumulative results of my over-two-decade study of Korean literature, history and culture. I have many teachers, colleagues and friends who have added to my knowledge of 'things Korean' and hope this work, in some small way, reflects the wisdom I have gained from these individuals over the years. I am also greatly indebted to many for assistance in collecting photographs, information, finding particular foods and so on. Moreover, I am certain that I inconvenienced many a fellow diner in photographing various foods and dishes before eating. Not a meal passed, it seems, without a lengthy session of positioning and photographing various dishes. However, due to their patience and hospitality, I have been able to complete this volume.

I would like to mention several individuals who helped me directly with this work. Cha Hye and Kwon Sungyong were very helpful in locating speciality restaurants and invested much time on my behalf. Sohn Youngsun was very kind to provide me photographs of difficult to find foods. Grace Hong of Binghamton University painstakingly prepared the various illustrations for this volume that have helped clarify some otherwise difficult concepts. Charlotte Horlyck of the University of London read through my manuscript and gave me very detailed suggestions for improvement which have greatly improved the final version. Gregory N. Evon of the University of New South Wales also read through some of my drafts and this work has benefited greatly from his thoughtful commentary. Finally, my wife, Cha Kil, has done a great deal of the leg work in taking pictures for this volume. Moreover, she has been, as always, an excellent sounding board for my ideas.

Reaktion Books has also been very helpful and supportive in the lengthy processes of preparing this manuscript. The various editors there have helped with all the technical aspects of preparing photographs and artwork for this volume. The three anonymous reviewers of this manuscript provided me great assistance with the content, style and factual information. The finished book is much better for their detailed and insightful comments.

This work is also indebted to some excellent materials compiled in Korea. The twenty-eight volume encyclopedia covering Korean culture published by the Academy of Korean Studies, *Han'guk minjok munhwa taebaekkwa sajŏn* ('Encyclopedia of Korean Culture'), was of tremendous help in my research, as was the volume on food culture published by the Institute of Korean Culture at Korea University, *Han'guk minsok ŭi segye* ('Survey of Korean Folk Culture'). Also important was the two-volume *Han'guk minsok taesajŏn* ('Encyclopedia of Korean Folk Culture'), for adding historic insight.

Any errors, omissions or oversights are, of course, the fault of this writer. I have endeavoured to be accurate and minimize any such flaws. I hope that this volume will help, in some small way, to open up the world of Korean cuisine and culture to others, and that they might enjoy them as I have.

Photo Acknowledgements

Photos by the author: pp. 11, 16, 18, 22, 25, 50, 78, 85, 93, 94 (top), 99, 103 (top), 105 (top), 107, 113, 114, 116, 117, 119, 120, 124, 129 (foot), 136, 143, 145, 146, 147, 148, 149, 150, 153, 154, 157; photos Cha Hye: pp. 95, 174 (top); from Ch'oi Mujang and Im Yŏnch'ŏl, eds, *Koguryŏ pyŏkhwa kobun* ('Tomb Murals of Koguryŏ') (Seoul, 1990): p. 12; photos Kil Cha: pp. 8, 9, 14, 23, 29, 30, 31, 32, 34, 35, 36, 38, 39, 46, 47, 49, 52, 53, 54, 55, 56, 58 (top, middle), 61, 63, 64 (foot), 66, 67, 71, 73, 74, 77, 80, 82, 84, 86, 89, 94 (foot), 96, 97, 100, 101, 103 (foot), 105 (foot), 108, 115, 122, 123, 125, 126, 127, 131, 133, 134, 137, 138, 139, 140, 161, 164, 167, 168, 170, 171, 173 (foot), 174 (foot), 175; photos from the Library of Congress, Washington, DC (Prints and Photographs Division): pp. 70 (LC-USZ62-72687), 121 (LC-USZ62-72649), 144 (LC-USZ62-79643); from National Museum of Korea, *Chosŏn sidae ŭi p'ungsokhwa* ('Folk Paintings of the Chosŏn Dynasty') (Seoul, 2002): p. 69; from National Museum of Korea, *Dynastic Heritage of Korea* (Seoul, 2002): p. 111; from Seoul Museum of History, *Seoul: Heaven, Earth, Man* (Seoul, 2002): pp. 28, 90, 129 (top); photos Sohn Youngsun: pp. 60, 64 (top), 173 (top), 176.

Index